LOOKING TO HIRE AN HR LEADER?

LOOKING TO HIRE AN HR LEADER?

14 Action Tools to Help You Decide, Find, and Keep the HR Professional Your Business Needs in a Competitive World

PHYLLIS G. HARTMAN, SPHR

Society for Human Resource Management
Alexandria, Virginia
www.shrm.org

Strategic Human Resource Management India
Mumbai, India
www.shrmindia.org

Society for Human Resource Management
Haidian District Beijing, China
www.shrm.org/cn

This book is published by the Society for Human Resource Management (SHRM®). The interpretations, conclusions, and recommendations in this book are those of the author and do not necessarily represent those of the publisher.

Founded in 1948, the Society for Human Resource Management (SHRM) is the world's largest HR membership organization devoted to human resource management. Representing more than 275,000 members in over 160 countries, the Society is the leading provider of resources to serve the needs of HR professionals and advance the professional practice of human resource management. SHRM has more than 575 affiliated chapters within the United States and subsidiary offices in China, India and United Arab Emirates. Visit us at shrm.org.

Interior and Cover Design: Jihee Kang Lombardi

Library of Congress Cataloging-in-Publication Data (on file)

ISBN 978-1-58644-367-2

Contents

To Chuck, my more serious other half without whom
I would not have been able to do anything significant in my HR career.

Preface

The purpose of this book is to provide business owners and managers with information that will enable them to make good decisions when hiring an HR professional. It includes processes and tools that can help in planning and evaluating the HR needs in any organization as well as charts, forms, and tips to make the recruiting and hiring process more effective.

The information in this book should make the process easier. The focus, however, is not on making the process quicker. Hiring too quickly often leads to hiring the wrong person or hiring for a job you do not need. Planning carefully takes time, but it is only through good planning that you are likely to get the best person for your organization.

This book is not a research report driven by data and statistical analysis, but it is based on the author's 25-plus years of experience in the profession and information from a number of respected sources on the HR profession. There are no guarantees that if you follow all the steps and use all the tools that you will recruit the perfect HR professional, but hopefully you will have favorable results and business success.

Why do I use the term "HR professionals" in the title and throughout the book rather than "HR managers?" In all likelihood you will be using the ideas in this book to hire an HR manager, someone who will provide expertise as a part of your management team. But you might consider hiring your HR professional for a range of titles in your organization, from a chief human resource officer to an HR coordinator, so I did not want to limit the information to only one title.

CHAPTER 1

What Does Human Resources Do?

Why Do I Need an HR Professional?

Worldwide business leaders are recognizing that the climate they operate in is constantly changing, and if they are focused on future success, they need to plan for their response. On popular websites and in blogs, magazines, and books, the same words—innovation, competitive advantage, problem-solving—keep coming up again and again. When managers talk about business challenges, the central themes of having the "right" employees, responding to changing laws and regulations, dealing with rapid technical change, and coping with global business can be heard over and over.

These trends are generally recognized to be a result of a number of factors, including instant communication driven by developments in technology, an aging skilled and educated workforce in developed countries and the failure of some education systems, revelations of unethical behaviors that have led to increased regulations and laws as well as lost revenue and legal costs, and a more closely connected global economy.

What is important to acknowledge is that the underlying factor that can influence a company's ability to respond to and survive the challenges is its people. You can, after all, create similar products and services or use materials, processes, and operations of the most successful companies, but what you cannot copy is the employees.

HR professionals, based on their knowledge and experience, are able to help balance the needs of the employees and the needs of the organization. Most management professionals, whether they are in operations, sales, finance, or other areas, are recognized as being "specialists" in their area. Their main focus is usually on their department or function, and their goals are to bring in profit or revenues so that the organization can be successful. It is not that they do not see the value of employees or do not care about who is working for them, but the employees are often just a part of their focus. Human resources, on the other hand, has a direct focus on the employees. Human resources is usually tasked with understanding what the organization expects and needs from its employees and then with determining how best to meet those goals by finding the right employees and working to engage them.

If I'm a Good People Manager, Why Do I Need an HR Professional?

If you are reading this book, you are likely considering hiring an HR professional and you are facing challenges when it comes to employees. These challenges may have nothing to do with your ability to manage people.

The problem is the business world is much more complex and competitive than it once was. Technology is driving access to a global market for customers and talent, and litigation trends are making it easier and more common for companies to be sued by employees.

The relationship between the employee and the employer has changed. Employee expectations and demands of an employer are the differences between an engaged and productive workforce and a struggling, high-turnover, dispassionate workforce.

Can you as the business owner/leader/manager proactively do all the HR functions that lead to better organizations while still being able to meet your own responsibilities?

Just as you would seek help from an attorney rather than represent yourself in court or from a physician when you are sick, doesn't it make sense to employ the insights and expertise of an HR professional?

HR professionals are tasked today with helping businesses establish and maintain a new relationship with employees. They need to understand how the business operates and also maintain the best strategies for dealing with employees. The HR function has become a specialized one that would be difficult for most general managers and managers to achieve. As a team, however, they can work together to make the organization successful.

What Does HR Do?

Simply stated, HR professionals, using a strong base of business knowledge, work with the organization to hire, engage, develop, and manage the employees.

There are some generally accepted HR functions that every organization needs at some level and the impacts that can occur if they are not effective. The Society for Human Resource Management (SHRM), a professional trade association, has developed a breakdown of HR functions.[1] Table 1.1 includes a compilation of some information from those documents.

TABLE 1.1 **HR FUNCTIONS IN ORGANIZATIONS**		
FUNCTION*	**WHAT HR DOES***	**HOW HR HELPS THE BUSINESS**
Business management and strategy	•Interprets internal business, external business, technical, economic, labor, and legal information and applies to HR and business •Establishes internal and external relationships to benefit the business •Aligns human capital planning with the business plans •Communicates and supports core business values •Monitors legislative and regulatory environment to respond to business impacts	•Insures strategic planning includes employee impacts •Contributes to expense controls for HR costs •Reduces losses from HR legal issues •Encourages employee support of the organization
Workforce planning and employment	•Determines what talent, skills, and competencies the business needs now and in the future •Manages documentation for job tasks and necessary skills, experience •Establishes sources for the best candidates •Manages recruitment /selection processes •Trains managers on effective selection •Ensures processes are legally compliant •Manages record-keeping for employment processes •Leads planning for job structures that attract desired candidates •Manages succession planning	•Reduces turnover costs •Reduces time to new employee effectiveness •Controls cost per hire and time to hire •Responds to and reduces complaints and legal actions •Controls recruiting and hiring costs •Improves employee morale •Reduces loss of productivity

CONTINUED →

TABLE 1.1 **HR FUNCTIONS IN ORGANIZATIONS**		
Compensation and benefits	• Develops salary strategies and budgeting that attract and keep the best employees • Ensures legal compliance • Maintains payroll processes • Establishes benefit strategies—direct cost and indirect cost • Communicates about pay and benefits to employees • Negotiates with benefits vendors • Deals with government-mandated benefits	• Maintains a positive ratio of pay to sales/profit • Ensures competitive pay/benefits that attract and retain top talent • Supports responses to retention and performance issues • Encourages employee participation in benefits that affects costs • Reduces the likelihood of fines, lawsuits, complaints • Controls benefits costs
Employee and labor relations	• Matches company culture and employee relations • Engages employees • Develops strategies that influence employee attitudes • Manages employee policies and procedures that are necessary, effective, and legally compliant • Deals with organized labor • Coaches managers and facilitates discipline and corrective actions • Deals with international and global issues related to hiring or sending workers to other countries • Requires affirmative action planning for some federal contractors	• Supports positive productivity • Controls turnover costs • Monitors, responds to, and analyzes number of formal complaints • Monitors, responds to, and analyzes number of complaints settled out of court • Controls/reduces legal costs • Leads responses to unionization efforts • Tracks and responds to time to resolution for grievances and bargaining in union environments • Responds to and tracks morale issues that lead to productivity issues • Raises awareness about workplace violence and its costs and leads programs to reduce risk
Employee development	• Develops and manages training/education programs • Oversees talent assessment and management • Engages in leadership development • Manages succession planning • Selects and implements required training • Manages organizational development—broad training needs and change management	• Controls training investment/costs • Ensures training that supports the organization's mission and goals • Measures return on investment (ROI) of training and development • Applies training to the right employees • Establishes training that encourages retention • Plans for and tracks employees who can replace or succeed leaders • Helps to control costs related to legal training compliance

CONTINUED →

TABLE 1.1 **HR FUNCTIONS IN ORGANIZATIONS**		
Risk management	•Manages safety programs •Coordinates security plans and policies •Manages return-to-work programs •Responds to workplace health issues •Keeps up with safety laws and regulations including the Occupational Safety and Health Administration (OSHA) and other legal requirements •Manages general liability and workers' compensation •Establishes and administers workplace ethics policies •Supports employee behaviors that ensure safety, security, and ethical behavior •Establishes emergency response and safety programs	•Addresses productivity issues by reducing lost work time due to injuries and illness •Responds to and controls OSHA and other agency fines •Controls workers' compensation costs •Negotiates and controls insurance rates •Tracks and responds to number of complaints and legal costs

* Source: Society for Human Resource Management, *2014 SHRM Learning System for PHR/SPHR Certification Preparation, Module 1: Business Management and Strategy* (Alexandria, VA: SHRM, 2014).

HR professionals may not manage all the functions in Table 1.1, depending on the specific organization or business. If safety is a significant issue for your business as is the case with some manufacturing companies, you may employee an individual that manages safety. But if you examine Table 1.1, you can see that there are connections between these functions, so the HR professional might assist with managing or planning training for safety procedures, for example.

The costs of ineffective HR functions may be obvious, but when we add numbers, it is clearer that good HR help may be a necessity.

The number of equal employment opportunity (EEO) charges—of discriminatory practices in the workplace—rose from 82,792 in 2007 to 99,412 in 2012, a 20 percent increase over five years.[2] This number does not include the damage awards from nongovernmental litigation. A quick look at the U.S. Equal Employment Opportunity Commission website "Newsroom" showed fines levied between April 2013 and March 2013 ran from $15,000 to $750,000 (not counting jury awards).[3]

The U.S. Department of Labor (DOL) administers and enforces more than 180 federal laws.[4] There are 50 percent more federal wage and hour investigators in early 2014 than in 2008; in the DOL's 2013 requested budget, the agency sought 1,839 full-time investigators.

Businesses should plan to devote 15 percent to 30 percent of their gross revenue to payroll, and according to Second Wind Consultants, businesses within this range tend to be the most successful.[5]

The advantage of having an HR professional with knowledge and experience, who can focus on and keep up with changes related to employee management, is that the other specialist managers (accounting, operations, sales, etc.) can focus on their areas and together have a more effective workplace.

In Chapter 2 we will discuss how you can define what your organization needs when it comes to HR help. Factors like the number of employees, the nature of the business, and the locations of employees and managers all help you determine if you need an HR professional and what skills, knowledge, and competencies that individual must have to help you be successful.

CHAPTER 2

Defining Organizational Needs

When there are employee problems—or the potential for them—it is easy to look for silver bullet solutions. But when you are considering hiring an HR professional or filling any other important position, do your homework first. If you do not really know what you want, how can you select the right person? Panic hiring is never a good approach as it will cost you money.

A survey conducted by Harris Interactive for CareerBuilder in 2012 revealed that more than 40 percent of U.S. employers estimated that a bad hiring decision had cost their companies more than $25,000. One-quarter of the respondents estimated the cost to be more than $50,000.[1]

This chapter will take you through a process to determine what HR services and functions you need. If you are familiar with strategic planning processes, this approach will be familiar. You need to define where your organization is now, where you want it to be, and what your HR function should look like to get you there.

Step 1. Do You Need an HR Professional?

You need to consider a number of factors when making this decision:

- How many employees do you have, and where are they? The general rule of thumb is that you need an HR professional if you have 90 to 100 employees.
- The location(s) of the employees and their supervisors, and the physical distance as well as the contact they have with each other, can add complexity to employee relations for your business.

7

- What is your core business type?
- Do you expect or are you planning major changes in your business in the near future?

Different businesses have different needs when it comes to employees. For example, if you provide services to your clients or customers, you may need to have employees with strong soft skills (for example, interpersonal communication, time management, empathy) as well as technical skills. You would need an HR professional who has the ability to evaluate and manage development of those skills. The more complex your business and the more impact the employees have on your success, the more likely that you need an HR professional.

Various industries or businesses may be more likely to have a history of organized labor or may be more probable targets for union organizing, like manufacturing or health care. If these factors come into play, you are more likely to need someone who can focus on employee relations or labor relations. Your HR professional would need to have knowledge and skills related to collective bargaining or union avoidance.

- What business challenges and changes are you likely to face in the next few years? Are you expecting to grow your business, or are you facing decline that will necessitate changes? How is your competition positioned? How likely is it that your top performers will still be with your organization in five years? Ten years? A simple and honest SWOT assessment of your business to look at strengths, weaknesses, opportunities, and threats may indicate that changes are coming soon. If you have a family-owned business, is a clear succession plan in place? Are you planning to acquire other businesses? How much turnover are you likely to have, and what kind of competition are you facing for skilled workers? Any of these factors will influence your need for an HR professional.

Decision Worksheet 2.1 (Do I Need an HR Professional?) will help you analyze the company information. (Decision worksheets can be found at the end of each chapter.) The points attached to the various aspects correlate to the information above. For example, if you have 90 to 100 employees, you *definitely* need an HR professional, and once you reach 300, you need an HR staff.

Three case studies applying this worksheet follow.

Case Study A: Small Community Bank

A small community bank with four branches has about 65 total employees. Currently the HR functions are being handled by the operations vice president. The payroll processing is outsourced, but data entry for time-keeping is done by an accounting assistant. The bank faces stiff competition from larger banks in the area for customers and employees. The majority of employees in teller and customer service positions are over 50 years old, and until recently turnover was quite low within this group. However, the turnover rate for newer, younger employees has been high, and finding qualified individuals who can pass drug tests and background checks has been increasingly difficult. Several older workers have had attendance issues, and they may be covered under the Americans with Disabilities Act (ADA). The bank is aware of the Family and Medical Leave Act (FMLA), but the operations VP is not sure how it applies and how it relates to the ADA. Reputation and legal compliance are critical in this business. Customer loyalty and community banking are the market strategy of the bank in competing with bigger banks. The bank hopes to remain stable in the next one to five years.

Using Decision Worksheet 2.1, the bank has determined that it would make sense to hire an HR professional (see Table 2.1).

TABLE 2.1 **DOES THE SMALL COMMUNITY BANK NEED AN HR PROFESSIONAL?**		
NUMBER OF EMPLOYEES	**POINTS**	**CHECK ALL THAT APPLY**
1-15	0	
16-50	2	
51-90	3	x
91-100	8	
100-300	10	
301+	15	
Total for number	**3**	
LOCATION OF EMPLOYEES	**POINTS**	
100% same location	0	
75% at the same site, 25% at one or more other sites	1	
50% at the same site, 50% at one or more other sites	2	
25% at the same site, 75% at one or more other sites	3	x
100% at a variety of sites	4	
Total for location	**3**	
BUSINESS FACTORS (SELECT ALL THAT APPLY)	**POINTS**	
Type of business		
Personal service—health care, education, social services	5	
Durable goods/materials—manufacturing, mining, construction	4	
Retail service—stores, food service, wholesale	4	
Transportation/warehousing—trucking, public transit, distribution	3	
Information—telecommunications, computer services	3	
Utilities—gas, electric, water/sewer	3	
Finance/insurance/real-estate	3	x
Government—public services and safety	2	
Expected changes		
Business growth in 1-5 years expected	3	
No business growth expected—stable business projections	1	
Business decline expected in 1-5 years—change needed	4	
Change in leadership or retirement of owner, expected in 1-5 years	4	
Expect to acquire/buy other business(es) in 1-5 years	4	
Employee turnover expected in 1-5 years	4	x
Strong competition for skilled employees—current or 1-5 years	4	x
Total for factors	**11**	

CONTINUED →

TABLE 2.1 DOES THE SMALL COMMUNITY BANK NEED AN HR PROFESSIONAL?			
TALLY			
NUMBER-OF-EMPLOYEES POINTS	LOCATION POINTS	BUSINESS FACTOR POINTS	YOUR TOTAL
3	3	11	17
ANALYZE YOUR RESULTS			
YOUR TOTAL	NEED FOR A FULL-TIME HR PROFESSIONAL	OTHER THOUGHTS	
1-9	Unlikely	Check out the U.S. Department of Labor laws and the labor laws in the state(s) you do business in. Use the Decision Worksheet 2.2. Establish a strong relationship with a labor attorney or HR consultant, and join and participate in a local chamber of commerce or business organization to stay up-to-date.	
10-14	Likely	Use Decision Worksheet 2.2 to begin planning for your HR function needs going forward.	
15 or more	Definitely	Use Decision Worksheet 2.2 to begin planning for hiring an HR professional.	

Source: Society for Human Resource Management, *2014 SHRM Learning System for PHR/SPHR Certification Preparation, Module 1: Business Management and Strategy* (Alexandria, VA: SHRM, 2014), ix-xvii.

The worksheet total is 17, which indicates that the bank should have an HR professional. Expected changes and the type of business, more than the number of employees, lead to the need.

Case Study B: Family-Owned Business

A family-owned manufacturing business has 220 employees in five in-state locations. There is no HR professional. The company has used a labor attorney, a labor relations attorney, and an HR consultant for contract negotiations and HR-related issues. In business for 75 years, the company has been successful in manufacturing products used as component parts by other manufacturers. The third generation of the family is beginning to take over the leadership roles. Two of the primary locations, which are manufacturing plants, have a large percentage of production workers who are approaching retirement. One of the locations is unionized; the others are not, and there have been recent rumors of a union-organizing campaign at a business in the area. The company is poised for growth through acquisition or addition of a sixth site. Production workers need specific skills that are not easily found. Until now, one of the second-generation leaders has handled all HR functions except for recruitment, which has been done primarily by local managers. This leader, who has other duties, is likely to retire in the next five years. No one in the current leadership is interested in assuming the HR functions.

Table 2.2 indicates whether this business needs an HR professional.

TABLE 2.2 DOES THE FAMILY-OWNED BUSINESS NEED AN HR PROFESSIONAL?		
NUMBER OF EMPLOYEES	**POINTS**	**CHECK ALL THAT APPLY**
1-15	0	
16-50	2	
51-90	3	
91-100	4	
100-300	5	x
301+	15	
Total for number	5	
LOCATION OF EMPLOYEES	**POINTS**	
100% same location	0	
75% at the same site, 25% at one or more other sites	1	
50% at the same site, 50% at one or more other sites	2	
25% at the same site, 75% at one or more other sites	3	
100% at a variety of sites	4	x
Total for location	4	
BUSINESS FACTORS (SELECT ALL THAT APPLY)	**POINTS**	
Type of business		
Personal service—health care, education, social services	5	
Durable goods/materials—manufacturing, mining, construction	4	x
Retail service—stores, food service, wholesale	4	
Transportation/warehousing—trucking, public transit, distribution	3	
Information—telecommunications, computer services	3	
Utilities—gas, electric, water/sewer	3	
Finance/insurance/real-estate	3	
Government—public services and safety	2	
Expected changes		
Business growth in 1-5 years expected	3	x
No business growth expected—stable business projections	1	
Business decline expected in 1-5 years—change needed	4	
Change in leadership or retirement of owner, expected in 1-5 years	4	x
Expect to acquire/buy other business(es) in 1-5 years	4	x
Employee turnover expected in 1-5 years	4	x
Strong competition for skilled employees—current or 1-5 years	4	x
Total for factors	23	

CONTINUED →

TABLE 2.2 DOES THE FAMILY-OWNED BUSINESS NEED AN HR PROFESSIONAL?

TALLY

NUMBER-OF-EMPLOYEES POINTS	LOCATION POINTS	BUSINESS FACTOR POINTS	YOUR TOTAL
5	4	23	32

ANALYZE YOUR RESULTS

YOUR TOTAL	NEED FOR A FULL-TIME HR PROFESSIONAL	OTHER THOUGHTS
1-9	Unlikely	Check out the U.S. Department of Labor laws and the labor laws in the state(s) you do business in. Use the Decision Worksheet 2.2. Establish a strong relationship with a labor attorney or HR consultant, and join and participate in a local chamber of commerce or business organization to stay up-to-date.
10-14	Likely	Use Decision Worksheet 2.2 to begin planning for your HR function needs going forward.
15 or more	Definitely	Use Decision Worksheet 2.2 to begin planning for hiring an HR professional.

Source: Society for Human Resource Management, *2014 SHRM Learning System for PHR/SPHR Certification Preparation, Module 1: Business Management and Strategy* (Alexandria, VA: SHRM, 2014), ix-xvii.

The worksheet total is 32, which indicates that the family-owned business should have an HR professional. The number of employees, industry type, and significant changes are the weighty factors here.

Case Study C: Elder Care and Nursing Business

The Happy Care Company has experienced significant growth as the Baby Boomer generation ages. Established as a small hospital-related nursing facility with 20 employees, it was sold two years ago to a private investor focused on growth. The company currently has 50 employees, many of whom are low-paid direct-care workers. There has been some challenge in finding individuals to work at the facility as it is critical that they have a strong work ethic, no criminal or drug history, and the ability to do difficult physical work assisting the residents. The owner is currently negotiating to acquire two more facilities in adjoining states, which would bring the total employee population to over 150 employees. The newly acquired facilities currently include nursing and elder care but also offer home care services. The managers of the new facilities are the owners and will be retiring, though most of the employees are expected to stay.

Table 2.3 indicates whether this business needs an HR professional.

TABLE 2.3 **DOES THE ELDER CARE AND NURSING BUSINESS NEED AN HR PROFESSIONAL?**		
NUMBER OF EMPLOYEES	**POINTS**	**CHECK ALL THAT APPLY**
1-15	0	
16-50	2	x
51-90	3	
91-100	4	
100-300	5	
301+	15	
Total for number	**2**	
LOCATION OF EMPLOYEES	**POINTS**	
100% same location	0	
75% at the same site, 25% at one or more other sites	1	
50% at the same site, 50% at one or more other sites	2	
25% at the same site, 75% at one or more other sites	3	
100% at a variety of sites	4	x
Total for location	**4**	
BUSINESS FACTORS (SELECT ALL THAT APPLY)	**POINTS**	
Type of business		
Personal service—health care, education, social services	5	x
Durable goods/materials—manufacturing, mining, construction	4	
Retail service—stores, food service, wholesale	4	
Transportation/warehousing—trucking, public transit, distribution	3	
Information—telecommunications, computer services	3	
Utilities—gas, electric, water/sewer	3	
Finance/insurance/real-estate	3	
Government—public services and safety	2	
Expected changes		
Business growth in 1-5 years expected	3	x
No business growth expected—stable business projections	1	
Business decline expected in 1-5 years—change needed	4	
Change in leadership or retirement of owner, expected in 1-5 years	4	x
Expect to acquire/buy other business(es) in 1-5 years	4	x
Employee turnover expected in 1-5 years	4	x
Strong competition for skilled employees—current or 1-5 years	4	x
Total for factors	**24**	

CONTINUED →

TABLE 2.3 **DOES THE ELDER CARE AND NURSING BUSINESS NEED AN HR PROFESSIONAL?**			
TALLY			
NUMBER-OF-EMPLOYEES POINTS	**LOCATION POINTS**	**BUSINESS FACTOR POINTS**	**YOUR TOTAL**
2	4	24	30

ANALYZE YOUR RESULTS		
YOUR TOTAL	**NEED FOR A FULL-TIME HR PROFESSIONAL**	**OTHER THOUGHTS**
1-9	Unlikely	Check out the U.S. Department of Labor laws and the labor laws in the state(s) you do business in. Use the Decision Worksheet 2.2. Establish a strong relationship with a labor attorney or HR consultant, and join and participate in a local chamber of commerce or business organization to stay up-to-date.
10-14	Likely	Use Decision Worksheet 2.2 to begin planning for your HR function needs going forward.
15 or more	Definitely	Use Decision Worksheet 2.2 to begin planning for hiring an HR professional.

Source: Society for Human Resource Management, *2014 SHRM Learning System for PHR/SPHR Certification Preparation, Module 1: Business Management and Strategy* (Alexandria, VA: SHRM, 2014), ix-xvii.

As you can see in this case the industry and the changes occurring in the business cause the higher total numbers. The small number of current employees might lead the owner to think she does not need an HR professional initially. However, the new acquisitions and the change in the services offered make HR help important. The other factor is that the company will be combining several cultures into one company, which takes HR expertise to go smoothly.

Step 2. What Functions Do You Need an HR Professional To Do?

The various functions usually included in human resources were reviewed in Chapter 1. Once you determine the need for an HR professional (if you scored 15 or higher on Decision Worksheet 2.1 (Do I Need an HR Professional?), you now need to decide what that individual might be responsible for in your organization.

It is helpful to do a self-analysis of your HR functions before deciding what the job description for HR will include. Chapter 3 will help you decide if you can outsource some of the HR functions, often some of the more tactical pieces, so that your HR professional can concentrate on your most critical needs.

Decision Worksheet 2.2 (HR Processes) will help you review you HR functions. The information you gather in this exercise will help you select someone with the right knowledge and skills, and it can be used to help the HR professional you hire get a jump start on his or her work.

Step 3. Analyze Your Results

Once you have completed the review, go back and count the number of total "No" or "Not sure" answers for each section. This will give you an idea about what functional areas are priority needs for your organization. Use Decision Worksheet 2.3 (Calculating HR Priorities) to record your totals, and check the corresponding box to the right to establish if the area is a priority in the HR function or if it is well established and should be included in the HR professional's job as part of the management team. We will use this information in Chapters 3 and 4.

You will be using these results to determine the qualifications and responsibilities for your HR professional's job description in Chapter 3. Decision Worksheet 2.3 (Calculating HR Priorities) helps you identify the areas you may be weak in, thus where you need HR help. You should also review your results and consider adding functions that do not show up as priorities if you expect major changes.

One example of how this worksheet can be useful is by applying it to the case studies above. In Case Study A: Small Community Bank, the president working with the VP may discover that the bank has a good handle on compensation and risk management as well as some training, given that it is a heavily regulated business that ties to these areas. Its weaker areas might be in benefits and performance because it does not have an HR professional to help in these areas. In addition, faced with recruitment challenges and turnover potential, the president and VP may want to focus on recruitment, new-hire orientation, and employee communication when they hire their HR professional.

In Case Study B: Family Owned Business, employee communication and recruitment may be priorities due to the hiring challenges and the union organizing risks.

In Case Study C: Elder Care and Nursing Business, all areas are priorities due to the acquisitions and the likelihood that Decision Worksheet 2.3 will show the company does not have many processes or policies in place now. It will need them as the owners grow the business.

By now you should have a good handle on what you have in place for your HR functions and how and if you need an HR professional to assist the organization by leading these areas.

You have also determined if you really need to hire an HR professional or if you can manage your employees effectively as is or by focusing on getting help with a few HR functions. In the next chapter you will learn how to determine if you should outsource some functions even if you need an HR professional. In all likelihood you will still need an HR professional if the results indicated that, but you may want the professional to concentrate on managing the functions versus doing all the tasks. Even the best HR generalist—an individual who is knowledgeable in all areas of HR—is stronger or weaker in one or another area.

Also, some of the more tactical tasks may be outsourced to a vendor that can do them more effectively or less costly for you compared to hiring more HR people (see Chapter 8). One example of that is payroll processing. Because payroll has become more complicated over the years with all the tax filings, regulations, etc., many if not most companies use a vendor that processes their payroll for them. Rather than having their HR professional have this detailed expertise in payroll, they have HR manage the relationship with the vendor company. Another example is recruitment: Companies that need to recruit an individual for a unique high-level position may want to work with a professional executive recruiter given that the HR professional may not have the time or resources to find specialized candidates.

DECISION WORKSHEET 2.1. **DO I NEED AN HR PROFESSIONAL?**		
NUMBER OF EMPLOYEES	**POINTS**	**CHECK ALL THAT APPLY**
1-15	0	
16-50	2	
51-90	3	
91-100	8	
100-300	10	
301+	15	
Total for number		
LOCATION OF EMPLOYEES	**POINTS**	
100% same location	0	
75% at the same site, 25% at one or more other sites	1	
50% at the same site, 50% at one or more other sites	2	
25% at the same site, 75% at one or more other sites	3	
100% at a variety of sites	4	
Total for location		
BUSINESS FACTORS (SELECT ALL THAT APPLY)	**POINTS**	
Type of business		
Personal service—health care, education, social services	5	
Durable goods/materials—manufacturing, mining, construction	4	
Retail service—stores, food service, wholesale	4	
Transportation/warehousing—trucking, public transit, distribution	3	
Information—telecommunications, computer services	3	
Utilities—gas, electric, water/sewer	3	
Finance/insurance/real-estate	3	
Government—public services and safety	2	
Expected changes		
Business growth in 1-5 years expected	3	
No business growth expected—stable business projections	1	
Business decline expected in 1-5 years—change needed	4	
Change in leadership or retirement of owner, expected in 1-5 years	4	
Expect to acquire/buy other business(es) in 1-5 years	4	
Employee turnover expected in 1-5 years	4	
Strong competition for skilled employees—current or 1-5 years	4	
Total for factors		

 CONTINUED →

DECISION WORKSHEET 2.1. **TALLY**			
NUMBER-OF-EMPLOYEES POINTS	**LOCATION POINTS**	**BUSINESS FACTOR POINTS**	**YOUR TOTAL**

DECISION WORKSHEET 2.1. **ANALYZE YOUR RESULTS**		
YOUR TOTAL	**NEED FOR A FULL-TIME HR PROFESSIONAL**	**OTHER THOUGHTS**
1-9	Unlikely	Check out the U.S. Department of Labor laws and the labor laws in the state(s) you do business in. Use the Decision Worksheet 2.2. Establish a strong relationship with a labor attorney or HR consultant, and join and participate in a local chamber of commerce or business organization to stay up-to-date.
10-14	Likely	Use Decision Worksheet 2.2 to begin planning for your HR function needs going forward.
15 or more	Definitely	Use Decision Worksheet 2.2 to begin planning for hiring an HR professional.

Source: Society for Human Resource Management, *2014 SHRM Learning System for PHR/SPHR Certification Preparation, Module 1: Business Management and Strategy* (Alexandria, VA: SHRM, 2014), ix-xvii.

DECISION WORKSHEET 2.2. **HR PROCESSES**			
Completed by:		**Date completed:**	
Data gathered from (list individuals or files used):			

EMPLOYEE COMMUNICATIONS AND DOCUMENTS	YES	NO	NOT SURE
A. Employee files			
1. Are there employee files? *If yes:*	☐	☐	☐
a. Are separate files for non-job/confidential information and I-9 forms maintained?	☐	☐	☐
b. Do you know who is responsible for employee files?	☐	☐	☐
c. Do you know who has access to the files?	☐	☐	☐
2. Is there an employee file policy/process?	☐	☐	☐
3. Is there a records retention policy/process?	☐	☐	☐
B. Employee handbook			
1. Is there an employee handbook or written employee policies?	☐	☐	☐
2. Are policies/handbook current and legally compliant?	☐	☐	☐
3. Do all employees have a copy?	☐	☐	☐
4. Do employees sign a receipt/statement saying they understand they are covered under the contents?	☐	☐	☐
5. Are supervisors trained in administering the policies?	☐	☐	☐
C. Employee communications			
1. Are there bulletin boards and a policy on who can use them?	☐	☐	☐
2. Is there a company intranet or social media sites and policies on employee use?	☐	☐	☐
3. Is there a complaint/grievance process in place?	☐	☐	☐
4. Is there an employee suggestion process?	☐	☐	☐
5. Are exit interviews done? *If yes:*	☐	☐	☐
a. Is the information from exit interviews acted on?	☐	☐	☐
6. Are there regular meetings with employees?	☐	☐	☐
7. Are legally required federal, state, and local posters/notices available for employees to see? *If yes:*	☐	☐	☐
a. Are federal posters/notices used?	☐	☐	☐
b. Are state posters/notices used?	☐	☐	☐
c. Are local posters/notices used?	☐	☐	☐
8. Do you conduct employee surveys at least once a year? *If yes:*	☐	☐	☐
a. Are the results kept confidential?	☐	☐	☐
b. Do you provide survey results to your employees?	☐	☐	☐
9. Do you have some/all of your employees sign nondisclosure and/or noncompete documents?	☐	☐	☐
Employee communications and documents total number of "No" and "Not sure" answers:			

 CONTINUED →

RECRUITMENT, EMPLOYMENT, AND SELECTION	YES	NO	NOT SURE
1. Are there recruitment and selection processes?	☐	☐	☐
2. Have interviewers been trained?	☐	☐	☐
3. Are hiring processes and decisions documented?	☐	☐	☐
4. Is any pre-employment testing being used? *If yes:*	☐	☐	☐
a. Is the testing valid, reliable, and nondiscriminatory?	☐	☐	☐
5. Are background investigations and reference checks being done? *If yes:*	☐	☐	☐
a. Are they consistently used, legal, and nondiscriminatory?	☐	☐	☐
6. Are less than 50% of positions filled from internal candidates?	☐	☐	☐
7. Are interview forms used?	☐	☐	☐
8. Are application forms used?	☐	☐	☐
9. Are offer letters used?	☐	☐	☐
10. Are rejection letters used?	☐	☐	☐
11. Are all forms reviewed by legal counsel?	☐	☐	☐
12. Are there job descriptions for every job? *If yes:*	☐	☐	☐
a. Are they current and accurate?	☐	☐	☐
b. Do they list the physical requirements of the job?	☐	☐	☐
13. Do employees participate in the development and review of their job descriptions?	☐	☐	☐
14. Is there a process in place to review and update job descriptions periodically?	☐	☐	☐
15. Is the hiring rate at your company expected to be 5% or less in the next three years, including expected turnover and growth?	☐	☐	☐
16. Do you have a list of regular external resources that you use to identify potential candidates (local newspaper help wanted, job boards, etc.)?	☐	☐	☐
17. Do multiple managers/supervisors interview each candidate?	☐	☐	☐
18. Is your annual voluntary turnover rate (the decision to terminate employment is the employee's) for managers less than 10%?	☐	☐	☐
19. Is your annual voluntary turnover rate (the decision to terminate employment is the employee's) for *nonmanagers* less than 10%?	☐	☐	☐
20. Do you have a policy and process that guards against discriminatory hiring practices?	☐	☐	☐
Recruitment, employment, and selection total number of "No" and "Not sure" answers:			

CONTINUED →

NEW-HIRE ORIENTATION	YES	NO	NOT SURE
1. Is there a new-hire or orientation process? *If yes:*	☐	☐	☐
a. Does it include filling out forms?	☐	☐	☐
b. Does it include review of the employee policies/handbook?	☐	☐	☐
c. Does it include meetings with the supervisor?	☐	☐	☐
d. Does it include on-the-job training?	☐	☐	☐
e. Does it include meetings with co-workers/team?	☐	☐	☐
2. Is there a buddy/mentor program for new hires?	☐	☐	☐
3. Is the hiring rate in the next five years expected to be less than 5%?	☐	☐	☐
4. Do you review the status of new hires 30, 60, and 90 days after the start date?	☐	☐	☐
New-hire orientation total number of "No" and "Not sure" answers:			

COMPENSATION AND WAGE ADMINISTRATION	YES	NO	NOT SURE
1. Are there defined pay processes?	☐	☐	☐
2. Do you know how the pay rates are determined?	☐	☐	☐
3. Are jobs classified as exempt versus nonexempt?	☐	☐	☐
4. Is there an annual increase process?	☐	☐	☐
5. Is equal pay provided for equal work?	☐	☐	☐
6. Are pay rates both externally and internally equitable and competitive?	☐	☐	☐
7. Has the company had legal counsel review pay practices for current and terminated employees?	☐	☐	☐
8. Are there bonuses or incentive payouts?	☐	☐	☐
9. Are there plan documents describing how the plans operate?	☐	☐	☐
10. Is incentive information communicated to employees?	☐	☐	☐
11. Is there a formal program to measure actual performance for short-term incentive purposes?	☐	☐	☐
12. Is time recorded and monitored for nonexempt jobs?	☐	☐	☐
13. Is there an attendance policy and procedure?	☐	☐	☐
14. Is there a no-call/no-show policy?	☐	☐	☐
15. Is there a reward for good attendance?	☐	☐	☐
16. Does employee pay account for less than 25% of total company expenses?	☐	☐	☐
17. Are there any reward or recognition programs available for employees beyond pay and bonuses?	☐	☐	☐
18. Do you communicate the "total compensation package" data to each employee?	☐	☐	☐
Compensation and wage administration total number of "No" and "Not sure" answers:			

CONTINUED →

BENEFITS	YES	NO	NOT SURE
1. Is there a policy regarding paid time off, vacations, holidays, sick days, and personal days?	☐	☐	☐
2. Is there a stated leave-of-absence policy? *If yes:*	☐	☐	☐
a. Do you know what it covers?	☐	☐	☐
b. Do you know how employees apply for a leave?	☐	☐	☐
c. Do you know who must approve leaves?	☐	☐	☐
d. Do you know how leaves are tracked?	☐	☐	☐
3. Is there compliance with laws pertaining to military leave, family and medical leave, pregnancy leave, disability leave, and workers' compensation leave?	☐	☐	☐
4. Do you offer health insurance?	☐	☐	☐
5. Do you offer life insurance?	☐	☐	☐
6. Do you offer dental insurance?	☐	☐	☐
7. Do you offer vision insurance?	☐	☐	☐
8. Do you offer an employee assistance program?	☐	☐	☐
9. Do you offer disability insurance?	☐	☐	☐
10. Do you offer flexible work scheduling?	☐	☐	☐
11. Of those benefits selected above (4-11) do you know which, if any, are voluntary?	☐	☐	☐
12. Do you know when benefits you offer become effective for your employees?	☐	☐	☐
13. Are premium contributions required of employees?	☐	☐	☐
14. Are all employees eligible for some coverage?	☐	☐	☐
15. Are summary plan descriptions given to employees?	☐	☐	☐
16. Are flexible benefits offered?	☐	☐	☐
17. Does the company comply with COBRA requirements?	☐	☐	☐
18. Does your company offer retirement benefits? *If yes:*	☐	☐	☐
a. Do you offer a traditional pension plan?	☐	☐	☐
b. Do you offer a 401(k) plan?	☐	☐	☐
c. Do you offer an IRA?	☐	☐	☐
19. Is your company ready to implement the employer's mandate under the Affordable Care Act and communicate the essential elements to your employees?	☐	☐	☐
20. Is information available to employees regarding workers' compensation policy and procedures?	☐	☐	☐
21. Do benefits costs account for less than 25% of total employee rewards (pay + benefits)?	☐	☐	☐
22. Has your company conducted a benefits audit within the past three years?	☐	☐	☐
Benefits total number of "No" and "Not sure" answers:			

CONTINUED →

SAFETY AND WELLNESS	YES	NO	NOT SURE
1. Are there safety policies and procedures that provide standards appropriate to the company/business?	☐	☐	☐
2. Is your business covered by OSHA regulations?	☐	☐	☐
3. In the last five years has your company been free of accidents/emergencies/violence that resulted in injuries or deaths?	☐	☐	☐
4. Does your company file an OSHA Form 300?	☐	☐	☐
5. Has your company had fewer than two workers' compensation issues in the last three years?	☐	☐	☐
6. Does your company provide regular safety training?	☐	☐	☐
7. Does your company have a process in place to respond to workplace emergencies or violence?	☐	☐	☐
8. Are the required and appropriate first-aid supplies available to employees?	☐	☐	☐
9. Do you offer wellness programs to employees?	☐	☐	☐
10. Do you have a workplace violence policy?	☐	☐	☐
11. Do you have a drug testing policy?	☐	☐	☐
12. Do you have a workplace bullying policy?	☐	☐	☐
Safety and wellness total number of "No" and "Not sure" answers:			

EMPLOYEE TRAINING AND DEVELOPMENT	YES	NO	NOT SURE
1. Is training provided for all employees?	☐	☐	☐
2. Do you know how employees are selected for training?	☐	☐	☐
3. Is pay for technical training courses, licenses, certification, and/or tuition reimbursement provided?	☐	☐	☐
4. Is there a written training policy?	☐	☐	☐
5. Is anyone responsible for tracking, budgeting, and coordinating training for employees?	☐	☐	☐
Employee training and development total number of "No" and "Not sure" answers:			

PERFORMANCE AND BEHAVIOR FEEDBACK PROCESSES	YES	NO	NOT SURE
1. Is a progressive discipline process/policy in place?	☐	☐	☐
2. Are there general work rules covering attendance?	☐	☐	☐
3. Are there general work rules covering absences?	☐	☐	☐
4. Are there general work rules covering tardiness?	☐	☐	☐
5. Are there general work rules covering theft?	☐	☐	☐
6. Are there general work rules covering alcohol and drug use?	☐	☐	☐
7. Are there general work rules covering insubordination?	☐	☐	☐
8. Are there general work rules covering confidentiality?	☐	☐	☐
9. Are there general work rules covering harassment?	☐	☐	☐
10. Are there general work rules covering hours of work?	☐	☐	☐

 CONTINUED →

PERFORMANCE AND BEHAVIOR FEEDBACK PROCESSES (CONTINUED)	YES	NO	NOT SURE
11. Are there general work rules covering meals and other breaks?	☐	☐	☐
12. Are there general work rules covering smoking?	☐	☐	☐
13. Are there general work rules covering dress code and personal appearance?	☐	☐	☐
14. Are there general work rules covering hiring of relatives?	☐	☐	☐
15. Are there general work rules covering workplace ethics?	☐	☐	☐
16. Are there general work rules covering conflicts of interest?	☐	☐	☐
17. Are there general work rules covering outside employment?	☐	☐	☐
18. Are there general work rules covering use of phone?	☐	☐	☐
19. Are there general work rules covering Internet use?	☐	☐	☐
20. Are there general work rules covering e-mail use?	☐	☐	☐
21. Are there general work rules covering voice mail use?	☐	☐	☐
22. Are there general work rules covering safety?	☐	☐	☐
23. Are there general work rules covering workplace violence?	☐	☐	☐
24. Is there a performance appraisal process? *If yes:*	☐	☐	☐
a. Does your company conduct periodic appraisals of performance for all employees with the results documented on a performance appraisal form?	☐	☐	☐
b. Do you know how often appraisals are done?	☐	☐	☐
c. Is the appraisal used to determine salary increases, pay grades, promotions, assignments, etc.?	☐	☐	☐
25. Is your performance appraisal linked to your company values?	☐	☐	☐
26. Is your performance appraisal linked to your company's strategic goals?	☐	☐	☐
27. Are employees provided annual goals that are SMART (specific, measurable, achievable, realistic, and time-bound) goals?	☐	☐	☐
Performance and behavior feedback processes total number of "No" and "Not sure" answers:			
TERMINATION PROCESSES	**YES**	**NO**	**NOT SURE**
1. Are terminable offenses documented?	☐	☐	☐
2. Are there written termination procedures?	☐	☐	☐
3. Is a specific person responsible for conducting terminations?	☐	☐	☐
4. Are there pay and benefits policies regarding terminated employees?	☐	☐	☐
5. Is there a system for responding to unemployment claims?	☐	☐	☐
6. Is there a rehire policy?	☐	☐	☐
7. Is the total turnover rate (voluntary and involuntary) less than 5%?	☐	☐	☐
Termination processes total number of "No" and "Not sure" answers:			

CONTINUED →

DECISION WORKSHEET 2.3. **CALCULATING HR PRIORITIES**					
A. FUNCTION/ ASPECT	**B. NUMBER OF "NO" OR "NOT SURE" ANSWERS**	**C. CRITERIA**	**D. PRIORITY IN HR**	**E. CRITERIA**	**F. INCLUDE IN HR**
Employee communication		If greater than 15 check next box		If greater than 8 check next box	
Recruitment, employment, and selection		If greater than 15 check next box		x	Always include
New-hire orientation		If greater than 4 check next box		If greater than 2 check next box	
Compensation and wage administration		If greater than 10 check next box		If greater than 8 check next box	
Benefits		If greater than 10 check next box		If greater than 5 check next box	
Safety and wellness		If greater than 5 check next box		If greater than 5 check next box	
Training and development		If greater than 2 check next box		If greater than 2 check next box	
Performance and behavior feedback		If greater than 5 check next box		x	Always include
Termination processes		If greater than 3 check next box		x	Always include

CHAPTER 3
Defining Candidate Qualifications and Creating the Job Description

Now that you have determined what components of HR you will be covering with your HR professional hire, it is time to zero in on the qualifications you need to look for to hire the right person. As you do that, you can create an appropriate job description. This chapter provides you with a discussion of qualifications and another Decision Worksheet that will be used to build your HR job description. We will also look at using the description to determine the pay range for your job.

Qualifications for HR Professionals

Qualifications include competencies, education, experience, and certifications a candidate has.

You can begin to define qualifications by looking at the tasks and responsibilities you expect your HR professional to carry out. Return to your completed Decision Worksheet 2.3 (Calculating HR Priorities). By examining the areas where you have the greatest need, you can begin to define the responsibilities of your HR professional.

Using Decision Worksheet 2.3, complete Section D (Functions) in Decision Worksheet 3.1 (Job Description). Functions by choosing those areas that make sense for your organization. Try to focus on the main responsibilities/functions. You may also be able to establish a title and reporting relationships in Sections A (Title) and B (Reporting Relationships).

This process will also drive the competencies, education, certification, and experience levels you will need.

HR Competencies

Competencies are characteristics that include knowledge, skills, traits, and ways of thinking that are demonstrated by behaviors. Though the concept has been around for a long time, the use of defined competencies in the workplace has become more popular in recent years. Competencies can be added to job descriptions and used in performance reviews to better define the job and the best candidate for the job. The Society for Human Resource Management (SHRM) has developed a competency model for HR professionals, and definitions used here are included with permission.[1]

It is useful to add appropriate competencies to your job description to help you (and your candidates) think about what the position requires in terms of behaviors. If you do this, you can look for people who have demonstrated those competencies through their behaviors in past jobs.

Though all the competencies listed in Decision Worksheet 3.1 (Job Description) might be considered important for any HR position, the level an individual needs varies based on the level of the position. Include the competencies that you know are particularly relevant to your position and organization. Think about the challenges facing your organization now and in the future. Consider your current management team and its strengths and weaknesses to determine competences that might add to the mix. Place your selections in Section I (Competencies) of Decision Worksheet 3.1.

Returning to the case studies in Chapter 2, the Small Community Bank (Case Study A) might identify HR expertise, relationship management, and communication as critical given that the bank has had an HR function managed by a non-HR professional, and it is challenged with turnover issues. The Family-Owned Business, in Case Study B, might focus on critical evaluation and relationship management due to the significant number of changes the company is undergoing. In Case Study C, the Elder Care and Nursing Business may want to choose leadership and navigation and business acumen because the new acquisitions add new business elements, and significant leadership changes will occur as the current owners retire.

Again, *all* competencies are valuable, but when selecting your HR professional, you will have needs that drive your selection focus.

Education and Experience

Next you need to consider how much education and experience your HR professional might need. If the individual is going to be leading the HR function and be responsible for overseeing a staff of other HR professionals, you will likely want him or her to have a minimum of a master's degree. However, education alone would not be enough for this role; experience would also be necessary. You should consider the education levels and combinations in your current management staff.

Because you are looking to your HR professional to bring you expertise, a bachelor's degree should be the minimum level of required education.

Types of degrees that are best for an HR professional besides HR management could include industrial relations or business as long as the course of study focuses on human resources or people management.

In terms of experience, again think about what you expect for other management positions. Less than five years of experience would likely not be enough to manage your HR function unless you have a small, stable organization.

The kind of experience you need goes back to what your areas of challenge are and what your expectations for change are going forward. For example, if you plan to do a lot of hiring and recruiting, you want someone who has that experience and skill.

It is wise to choose levels of education and experience to start with based on Decision Worksheet 3.3 (Calculating HR Priorities) results, but be willing to consider changing as you go through the recruiting process. You may ask for someone with a master's degree and five years of experience but find those individuals are at a pay range you cannot afford. Or you might find a great candidate with a bachelor's degree in a specific area and eight years of experience.

On Decision Worksheet 3.1 (Job Description) select education and experience levels in Sections E (Education) and F (Experience).

Professional Certifications

Professional certifications are more common in the HR field than they were in the past. Much as a certified accounting professional (CPA) indicates that the individual possesses knowledge in accounting principles and practices, HR certifications indicate that an individual possesses in-depth knowledge. Certifications go beyond college degrees in that they are specific to the area they include, and they tend to be more rigorous assessments. Most require individuals to pass a test or a series of tests, and they usually include a continuing education requirement if an individual wants to retain the certification.

For example, the PHR or Professional in Human Resources designation three-hour test can only be taken by individuals who have a minimum level of education and experience.[2]

Keep in mind that the certification does not necessarily guarantee that the individual can apply knowledge, but some higher-level tests (like the Senior Professional in Human Resources, or SPHR) do include application questions. Asking for a specific certification in your job description can serve as another filter to help you find the right person.

A sampling of current certifications is provided in Table 3.1. There are other, more specific certifications that may apply to specialized positions, but those listed in the table are generally recognized in the HR community.

TABLE 3.1 **A SAMPLE OF HR CERTIFICATIONS**		
CERTIFICATION	**GOVERNING BODY**	**DESCRIPTION**
SHRM-Certified Professional (SHRM-CP)	Society for Human Resource Management (shrm.org)	Built on one singular Body of Competency and Knowledge (BoCK) designed to elevate the HR profession around the world. It tests the HR professional's competency—the ability to put that knowledge to work through critical thinking and application. It demonstrates that the HR professional is a technical expert and has mastered the application of HR technical and behavioral competencies, through practice and experience, to drive business results.
SHRM-Senior Certified Professional (SHRM-SCP)	Society for Human Resource Management (shrm.org)	Built on one singular Body of Competency and Knowledge (BoCK) designed to elevate the HR profession around the world. It tests the senior HR professional's competency—the ability to put that knowledge to work through critical thinking and application. It demonstrates that the senior HR professional is a technical expert and has mastered the application of HR technical and behavioral competencies, through practice and experience, to drive business results.

CONTINUED →

TABLE 3.1 **A SAMPLE OF HR CERTIFICATIONS**		
Professional in Human Resources (PHR®)	HR Certification Institute (www.hrci.org)	Demonstrates mastery of the technical and operational aspects of HR practices and U.S. laws and regulations. The PHR is for the HR professional who focuses on program implementation, has a tactical/logistical orientation, is accountable to another HR professional within the organization, and has responsibilities that focus on the HR department rather than on the whole organization.
Senior Professional in Human Resources (SPHR®)	HR Certification Institute (www.hrci.org)	For those who have mastered the strategic and policy-making aspects of HR management in the United States. It is designed for the HR professional who plans HR policy, focuses on the "big picture," has ultimate accountability in the HR department, has breadth and depth of knowledge in all HR disciplines, understands the business beyond the HR function, and influences the overall organization.
Certified Professional in Human Resources and Compensation (CPHRC)	World Federation of Personnel Management Associations (WFPMA), in conjunction with member national associations including the Society for Human Resource Management and the Chartered Institute of Personnel and Development (CIPD)	Compensation material is drawn from the specific Body of Knowledge in Remuneration Management as identified by WorldatWork (formerly American Compensation Association).
Certified Compensation Professional (CCP)	WorldatWork Society of Certified Professionals (www.worldatworksociety.org)	Informs and tests managers who specialize in accounting, finance, and marketing with an objective set of exams.
Certified Professional in Learning and Performance Certification (CPLP)	Association for Talent Development (ATD) (www.astd.org)	Measures knowledge and practical expertise that can be applied to training responsibilities in HR.

Next, complete Decision Worksheet 3.1, Section G, for professional certification(s) you might want your HR professional to have. Given that some certifications are newer and that many years of experience and upward movement in a career may indicate a similar level as a certification, it may be wise to consider certifications as "desired" rather than as "required" components.

Professional Memberships

Individuals who maintain membership in a professional organization involved in human resources demonstrate a commitment to their profession. In addition, being involved with other HR professionals gives them resources to find answers that can benefit your organization. Most of these organizations also have an affiliation with certifying bodies and provide various educational opportunities to members.

You will probably want to include the appropriate organization in your criteria for an HR professional. Some of the more recognized HR organizations are listed in Table 3.2.

TABLE 3.2 **HR PROFESSIONAL MEMBERSHIP ORGANIZATIONS**	
ORGANIZATION	**DESCRIPTION**
Society for Human Resource Management (SHRM) (national/local) www.shrm.org	SHRM is the world's largest HR membership organization devoted to HR management. Representing more than 275,000 members in over 160 countries, the Society is the leading provider of resources to serve the needs of HR professionals and advance the professional practice of HR management. SHRM has more than 575 affiliated chapters within the United States and subsidiary offices in China, India, and United Arab Emirates.
Association for Talent Development (ATD) www.astd.org	ATD is the world's largest association dedicated to the training and development profession. ATD's members come from more than 100 countries and connect locally in more than 120 U.S. chapters and with more than 10 international strategic partners. Members work in thousands of organizations of all sizes, in government, as independent consultants, and as suppliers.
WorldatWork www.worldatwork.org	WorldatWork is a nonprofit HR association for professionals and organizations focused on compensation, benefits, work/life effectiveness, and total rewards—strategies to attract, motivate, and retain an engaged and productive workforce. WorldatWork and its affiliates provide comprehensive education, certification, research, advocacy, and community, enhancing careers of professionals and, ultimately, achieving better results for the organizations they serve. WorldatWork has more than 65,000 members and subscribers worldwide; 95 percent of Fortune 500 companies employ a WorldatWork member. Founded in 1955, WorldatWork is affiliated with more than 70 local HR associations.

CONTINUED →

TABLE 3.2 **HR PROFESSIONAL MEMBERSHIP ORGANIZATIONS**	
International Society of Certified Employee Benefit Specialists (ISCEBS) www.iscebs.org	ISCEBS is the premier interactive community providing educational resources, innovative thinking, and collective wisdom to help members excel and prosper in their careers. This membership organization is for those who have earned the Certified Employee Benefit Specialist (CEBS), Group Benefits Associate (GBA), Retirement Plans Associate (RPA), and Compensation Management Specialist (CMS) designations.

As with certifications, new or more appropriate professional organizations might be included. There may be non-HR organizations specific to your industry that may have HR interest groups or components. Memberships in these may help your HR professional stay up-to-date with your industry and stay connected.

Include the professional memberships you decide are appropriate in Section H of Decision Worksheet 3.1.

By now you have a completed Decision Worksheet 3.1 to use to create a job description for your HR professional.

When using this worksheet, keep in mind that the suggestions are just starting points. You may want to decrease or increase the responsibilities described depending on your needs for the HR professional. In addition, after you hire your employee, you may find that the individual has talents, experience, or skills that require you to change the description based on your business needs.

Now you can transfer the information from Decision Worksheet 3.1 to your job description format.

Benchmarking Your Description

One way to benchmark your description is to search employment websites for similar jobs to see what your competition for talent is looking for in HR professionals. Some resources include SHRM, LinkedIn, Monster, and TheLadders, which have listings that can give you ideas.

Once you have a description written, you need to determine what you will offer to pay for this position. There are several important steps here.

Salary Considerations

Determining Pay Range—Where Does This Position Fit in Your Organization?

If your job title is HR assistant and the position reports to a manager and does the tactical aspects of human resources, it would likely be a nonexempt position and be paid an hourly rate. Most likely, your HR professional position will be managing some or all of the HR functions and be an exempt position paid a salary.

Looking at how much you are paying others who are above, below, or at the same level as the position will help give you an idea of what you should pay. In addition, you want to determine how critical this position is to the future success of the organization. You may want to pay at a higher level to "hire" critical expertise. Or maybe you have been doing many of the HR functions and you need someone to help so you can move on to others areas of management. In this case you might be able to hire a less experienced, less educated HR professional who can grow into the job.

How Much Do Others Pay?

Next you should do some market research to determine what other employers are paying. When you compare your job to others, focus on the job duties and responsibilities rather than on the job title. A title may be unique to an industry or company size. A vice president in a small company may be compensated at a lower level than one in a large company. Banks have many assistant vice president positions, so the pay rate may not be appropriate to another industry.

Some sources of information are free like the U.S. Bureau of Labor Statistics (BLS).[3] The data available from BLS may be somewhat dated, so you should look at when the data were gathered and possibly increase the numbers by the cost of living increase since that date. In addition, the data may not be specific to your geographic area. The same job in California, where the cost of living is high, may be paid more than in South Carolina, where the cost of living is lower.

Websites like Salary.com may have information on pay ranges, but keep in mind the data on these sites is based on contributions from people on a voluntary basis, not on scientific research or vetted information, so it may not be accurate.

Professional organizations like SHRM may have salary data available, though unless you are a member, there may be a fee charged for the information. Even if you are not a member of SHRM, you can sign up for a free compensation newsletter through the SHRM Compensation and Benefits Topic Area online.[4]

You can contact a compensation firm and ask for data from large salary surveys it has access to, but again this may cost something. It may be worth a small investment, however, to test your pay rate.

If you belong to a local chamber of commerce or industry organization, it may have salary survey data you can access. Interest groups on LinkedIn or other business networking groups might release information or have articles that give information about pay rates.

By gathering numbers from at least three different sources and then comparing them you can get a starting point for your pay range.

Decision Worksheet 3.2 (Salary) will help you gather and organize the information.

Now that you have a good description and an idea about how much you want to pay, you can begin your search. It may seem that we are spending a lot of time in planning, but doing solid groundwork will save you time and money in the long run.

In the next two chapters we will explore how to find candidates and how to select the best one for your position.

DECISION WORKSHEET 3.1. **JOB DESCRIPTION**		
COMPONENT	**OPTIONS**	**CHECK ALL THAT APPLY**
A. Title	**HR generalist** Though generalists may exist at many levels, the title is often used to describe a position that is responsible for most if not all aspects of the HR functions but is not considered a manager.	
	HR specialist Specialists can exist at various levels, but the title is used to describe a position that takes care of one or a small group of functions and is combined with identification of the area; for example: HR benefits and compensation specialist.	
	HR coordinator Describes a generalist who may work with various other individuals in HR or managers but is not a manager level.	
	HR manager Responsible for HR functions, usually a generalist; may or may not oversee/manage other positions but is on the same level as other organization managers.	
	HR director Usually a higher-level HR manager often overseeing a number of HR professionals.	
	HR vice president High-level HR professional who manages the functions of HR.	
	Chief HR officer Highest-level HR professional typically in a larger organization.	
B. Reporting Relationships	Reports to president, CEO, or owner. Recommended that the top HR professional report to the top manager to ensure effectiveness of the role. Most critical if the title is "manager" or above.	
	Reports to HR manager/VP/CHRO, CFO, controller, operations manager, or VP, or other high-level manager.	
	Manages HR generalists, specialists, and coordinators in larger organizations.	
	Manages HR administrator and assistant.	
	Manages receptionist and scheduler.	
	Manages HR vendors.	

CONTINUED →

COMPONENT	OPTIONS	CHECK ALL THAT APPLY
C. General Description	Directly responsible for the overall administration, coordination, and evaluation of the HR functions.	
	Under general supervision performs HR administrative work.	
	Performs advanced, specialized, and administrative duties in designated HR program or area. Responsible for providing high-level support in the administration of an HR program.	
	Responsible for directing all of the people functions of the organization in accordance with the policies and practices; also responsible for the strategic HR planning.	
D. Functions	Maintains up-to-date knowledge of external business, technical, economic, legal, and labor issues and applies to HR and business planning.	
	Participates in organization strategic planning with other managers contributing HR aspects/considerations.	
	Establishes HR budgets including projections and manages those budgets.	
	Works with established HR budgets.	
	Supports organization mission, vision, and values; bases HR policies on them, includes them in performance goals, and communicates to and educates employees about them.	
	Develops/assists in creation and implementation of personnel policies and procedures; prepares and maintains employee handbook and policies and procedures manual.	
	Participates in developing department goals, objectives, and systems.	
	Establishes and administers compensation program and processes and revises as necessary.	
	Performs benefits administration to include vendor selection, claims resolution, change reporting, approving invoices for payment, and communicating benefits information to employees.	
	Administers employee benefits programs, including enrolling employees, resolving problems, and communicating with employees.	
	Develops and maintains affirmative action program; files EEO-1 report annually; maintains other records, reports, and logs to conform to EEO regulations.	
	Conducts recruitment effort for all exempt and nonexempt personnel and temporary employees; conducts new-employee orientations; monitors career-pathing program; writes and places advertisements.	

CONTINUED →

COMPONENT	OPTIONS	CHECK ALL THAT APPLY
D. Functions (continued)	Handles employee relations counseling, disciplinary activities, outplacement counseling, and exit interviewing.	
	Assists in evaluation of reports, decisions, and results of department in relation to established goals. Recommends new approaches, policies, and procedures to effect continual improvements in efficiency of department and services performed.	
	Maintains human resource information system (HRIS) records and compiles reports from database.	
	Enters data into HRIS system or available data management tools.	
	Maintains compliance with federal, state, and local regulations concerning employment.	
	Manages selection of vendors for HR services and manages provided services.	
	Manages the performance review process, establishing and updating processes and forms, educating employees and managers, and overseeing the application of the process.	
	Manages the labor relations and union relationships, including working with legal counsel and managers to resolve grievances and participate in collective bargaining.	
	Manages training and development programs and activities for employees, including tuition reimbursement, internal training coordination, and on-the-job training.	
	Participates in management team workforce planning.	
	Manages HR function vendors, including working with management to source, select, and manage the performance of vendors (tracking, problem resolution, etc.).	
E. Education	A.S. in HR or business	
	B.S. in HR, industrial relations, business, management	
	M.S. in HRM, industrial relations, organizational development, management	
	MBA	
	Ph.D. in business	
F. Experience	This area should be determined based on specific needs identified in your analysis in previous chapters—benchmarking with other companies can help here. This list includes the typical ranges.	
	Internship in HR	
	1-3 years of generalist experience, or specialist in _____	

CONTINUED →

COMPONENT	OPTIONS	CHECK ALL THAT APPLY
F. Experience (continued)	3-5 years of generalist experience, or specialist in _____	
	5-10 years of generalist experience, or specialist in _____	
	10+ years of generalist experience, or specialist in _____	
G. Professional Certifications	Professional in Human Resources (PHR)	
	Senior Professional in Human Resources (SPHR)	
	Certified Compensation Professional (CCP)	
	Certified Professional in Human Resources and Compensation (CPHRC)	
	Certified Professional in Learning and Performance Certification (CPLP)	
	Others: _____	
H. Professional Memberships	Society for Human Resource Management (SHRM) (national/local)	
	Association for Talent Development (ATD)	
	WorldatWork	
	Society of Professional Benefit Administrators	
	Others: _____	
I. Competencies[a]	HR expertise The ability to apply the principles and practices of HR management to contribute to the success of the business.	
	Relationship management The ability to manage interactions to provide service and support to the organization.	
	Consultation The ability to provide guidance to organizational stakeholders.[b]	
	Leadership and navigation The ability to direct and contribute to initiatives and processes within the organization.	
	Communication The ability to effectively exchange with stakeholders.[b]	

CONTINUED →

COMPONENT	OPTIONS	CHECK ALL THAT APPLY
I. Competencies[a] (continued)	Diversity and inclusion The ability to value and consider the perspectives and backgrounds of all parties.	
	Ethical practice The ability to support and uphold the values of the organization while mitigating risk.	
	Critical evaluation The ability to interpret information to make business decisions and recommendations.	
	Business acumen The ability to understand and apply information to contribute to the organization's strategic plan.[c]	

[a] Based on a conversation the author had with Kari R. Strobel, director of HR Competencies, Society for Human Resource Management. Options for this section are included with permission from the SHRM HR Competency Model definitions.

[b] Organizational stakeholders may include employees, managers and supervisors, vendors, customers, clients, the community, and anyone who might be affected by the actions of the organization.

[c] Though all organizations should have a strategic plan, if yours does not have one, this competency would still be valuable in any business planning or forward planning that you do.

DECISION WORKSHEET 3.2 **SALARY**		
CONSIDERATIONS		
Reports to title	Pay range	Notes
Subordinate title(s)	Pay range	
This position	Range based on above data —	
RESEARCH GATHERED		
Source	Ranges	Notes
BLS		
WEBSITES (SALARY.COM, ETC.)		

CONTINUED →

FORMAL DATA (SHRM, ORGANIZATIONS, CONSULTING FIRMS)		
OTHER		
Starting range determined		

CHAPTER 4 Recruiting

In this chapter we will review sourcing strategies and resources, including how to use a professional recruiting firm, a temp agency, job boards (like iHireHR),[1] networking, professional organizations (like SHRM's HR Jobs),[2] and social networking.

If you have followed the previous chapters' processes, you now know that you want to find an HR professional, what that position includes, and what you think the candidates will need to have to be able to do the job. All of this planning will help as you now know what to look for.

The first step is to "source" or find candidates who match your needs.

What Is Most Important?

Keep in mind, however, that even if you know your criteria for an HR professional, there is never a perfect candidate. Go back to your job description, and prioritize the factors, so you can focus on the most critical aspects. For example, if you want a professional with five years of experience in benefits administration and a master's degree in HR and expertise in recruiting, you should weigh the three criteria so you can prioritize them. You may want to get other top managers involved in helping you determine what criteria are most desirable.

What's Your Recruiting Expertise?

Once you have your list of priorities, including the competencies you need, it is helpful to assess your own level of experience in sourcing and recruiting candidates.

If you have several years of successfully hiring experienced professionals and you have a well-developed recruiting process, you will likely start on your own. If, however, you have limited experience or no hiring process, you might want to work with a search firm or recruiting agency to source candidates.

Going It on Your Own

Create a Posting

Your posting is the ad for the position. To create a positive impression, your posting for an HR professional should be clear and accurate; after all, these individuals most likely know what should be included in an effective ad.

As you may already be aware, a good ad or posting has these components:
- Location of the job—including information on the need to visit multiple locations if that is part of the job.
- Basic/most important job tasks/responsibilities.
- Required education and skills.
- Information about the company, but you usually want to include the company name, a brief description of what the company does, and the company's website).
- Benefits of the job—you do not need to list specific medical benefits, but you might want to point out your company's employee privileges, like "free parking" or "onsite gym," to attract candidates.
- How to apply, an e-mail address, and website (if candidates can apply there); a regular mail address or fax number can also be included.
- Criteria for applying, which may include a requests for salary history or a resume and cover letter.
- A notation that you are an equal opportunity employer—all companies should be.

As in any posting, it is helpful to include attention-getting components. Job characteristics that may interest the general population may not be as appealing to HR professionals. According to a recent job satisfaction survey, opportunities to use their skills and abilities and the relationship with their immediate supervisor ranked one and two in importance for HR professionals.[3] Communication between employees and senior managers and autonomy and independence were also rated high. Keeping these features in mind and including them as appropriate in your posting are likely to attract the candidates you want.

If you have a marketing department or use professional marketing help, you might seek help in developing a posting. The marketing department or firm will likely have knowledge of the branding strategy used to sell your company's products and services and may be able to help you apply that information to you recruitment posting.

Examples of thorough postings are offered in Table 4.1.

TABLE 4.1. SAMPLE POSTINGS FOR HR POSITIONS

HR COORDINATOR
CDE Company is looking for an HR generalist who is interested in working closely with his or her boss to apply HR knowledge and skills to coordinate HR functions for 130 employees in a service company. If you have HR education and/or experience and an associate degree, this may be the job for you. The position includes maintaining records, assisting employees with signing up for benefits, maintaining HR policies, and working with company management. We provide competitive pay and good benefits plus a suburban setting with free parking. To apply, send your resume and pay history to zzz@CDE.com. EOE

HR MANAGER
Looking for a challenging HR generalist position in an organization that is committed to a positive, friendly culture? XYZ Bank (www.xyzbank.com) operates on the principle that banking is a people business, offering more choices in financial products and services, with a personal touch. As the HR manager you can support this culture by serving employees as internal customers and participating as part of the employee/management team. Located in Happy Hills, with 5 branches, XYZ is seeking an HR generalist. We have an onsite exercise program and free parking. You need a bachelor's degree in HR, business, or related field and at least 5 years of HR experience; PHR/SPHR desired. Experience in employee relations, talent acquisition, and organizational development required. Up-to-date knowledge of applicable legal issues required. If you have strong people skills, initiative, ability to work as a part of a team with management, and a demonstrated commitment to ethical practices, apply to XYZ HR at xyzhr@xyzbank.com. We are proud to be an EEO/AA employer M/F/D/V. NO CALLS.

EMPLOYEE RELATIONS SPECIALIST
Do you like the challenge of preventing and solving employee relations issues? Like working in a team-oriented environment as part of a top-notch HR department in a robust and growing company? Then this may be the job for you. ABC is looking for an ER Specialist. We seek creative individuals of the highest caliber who are interested in a work atmosphere based on teamwork, communication, and technical challenge. We offer a full benefits package, 401(k) plan, and tuition reimbursement. The ER Specialist develops and administers programs that promote positive employee relations and ensures compliance with federal, state, and company regulations. This includes investigating issues, providing guidance and recommendations for problem resolution, developing/maintaining communication programs, and supporting company-wide HR programs and initiatives. The ER Specialist also provides key coaching and support to supervisors and managers. If you have BS/BA in HR or business + 5-7 yrs exp, broad knowledge of progressive employee and labor relations, state and federal laws, knowledge of developing and implementing company policies/procedures/handbook, strong interpersonal skills, and can travel occasionally domestically, apply to: www.ABCco.com.

Set a Budget

Determine how much you want to spend on postings. Many sites may be free or inexpensive, but committing up to $300 is not unreasonable when recruiting for a professional. In addition, budget for background check services—usually between $60 and $120. If you plan to use any type of assessment or drug testing, you should consider that, too.

Where to Post/Advertise

If you are planning on recruiting on your own, research the best sites for posting HR positions. Just because a website has worked for recruiting a truck driver, it may not work to find an HR professional.

When posting any open position, consider your audience and where it might look for jobs or get information. In the case of HR professionals, it is reasonable to assume that they might look on HR or general websites or use certain social media sites. More senior professionals and those in traditional industries like banking or manufacturing, for example, are likely to use sites like Monster or LinkedIn. Younger professionals, who may be at entry level, might use Craigslist or Facebook to look for jobs. You need to look at your position and the likely candidates to decide where to start.

Today, the Internet, not the local newspaper, is where most people look for jobs. That said, there are large general sites that may attract good candidates if you want to look outside your geographic area. Local sites and organizations are better if you hope to recruit from your area.

The best approach is to go with the most targeted sites—those that reach your HR audience. It is not usually necessary to post on multiple sites to start with. If you are not getting results, then extend your reach.

Useful places to post may include professional HR organizations such as SHRM, the Association for Talent Development (ATD), formerly American Society for Training and Development (ASTD), the American Payroll Association (APA), and the International Foundation of Employee Benefit Plans. They have posting sites and tend to reach HR professionals directly.

Local chapters of professional organizations also often provide posting sites or information for their members. Sometimes these sites offer free or low-cost postings. In addition, the local networks of HR professionals may be well linked, and your job ad will get wide circulation.

Specific HR Internet job sites may also be effective, but make sure you evaluate the cost versus the benefit. Research the success they have or the results by looking at posted information or by calling them to ask about their success statistics. The time it takes to fill positions, the length of time that people stay, and the typical numbers of leads generated are all meaningful indicators. Talking to colleagues in the same industry about their experiences or looking for public reviews can give you information, too. When using review sites, look closely at the details and statistics rather than just assume that a large number of positive reviews means that a site is good.

Each state has a free "one-stop" workforce center providing services for both employers and employees. You can find these centers by checking your state government's website or the federal job site, USAJOBS.[4]

Colleges that have HR degree programs can be a good place to post, too. Even if you are not looking for an entry-level professional, many colleges have active alumni groups or networks. Contact local school career offices or HR departments to see how they can help you. They are usually cooperative because they want to maintain their reputation for having students who get jobs. Schools that offer graduate HR degree programs are usually a great source for talent.

Outplacement firms are another place to look for professionals. By posting your position with them or notifying them of an opening in HR, you reach people who may have been laid off as well as the network of HR professionals who the firm works with. Keep in mind that these firms cost the client company money to assist laid-off individuals, so the people being laid off are usually quality, valuable individuals.

Other Places to Look

Using networks is also a great way to look for HR professionals. Does your business network include companies that employee HR professionals? If so, why not talk to business colleagues about where they found their HR professional?

Setting up a booth at a job fair may not make sense if you are looking to hire one HR professional, but consider the fact that many if not most of the people staffing the booths there will be HR professionals. Job fairs may be a good resource if you are hiring for multiple other positions, too. You may want to attend just to network with other professionals.

Networking at business events or even at HR organization workshops or meetings may also net you some candidates, though the time involved may be prohibitive.

Finally, though print media may not be as popular for recruiting today, if you are in a geography where people still read the local paper, consider posting an ad there. Most print newspapers also have agreements with online services, so you may get more bang for your buck.

Social Networks

Though there are some legal risks in using social networks in business, their use especially for recruitment is the wave of the future. As noted above younger professionals are more likely to look to social networks, and as they move up in organizations, businesses will most likely continue to use the Internet.

According to a 2011 survey by SHRM, most HR professionals use LinkedIn to advertise for positions they are recruiting for. It would follow then that they might look there for jobs.[5]

LinkedIn and some other social networks, like SHRM Connect, that are business-focused are worth using. Though the truly "social" sites may be read by HR professionals, they may not convey the most professional image of your company.

Some sites offer paid posting services like LinkedIn. In addition, by searching such sites you might find interest groups that you can join or post to. These groups are made up of HR professionals, some who may be looking for a position. Often professionals are looking for a new opportunity while they are still working, and this is a way to connect with them.

Facebook and Twitter are also currently used by companies to promote their businesses. If you have a business Facebook or Twitter presence, both may be good places to advertise your HR position, particularly if you think the audience you are seeking uses it.

There are some risks, though, in using Facebook, Twitter, or other truly social sites.

In the case of Facebook, you probably want to avoid researching candidate information because the information posted may not be accurate and people post things that are not business-related, whereas LinkedIn is a business-focused site. Though seeing personal information may give insights into how potential candidates would fit into company cultures or might be clues as to the kind of person they are, you might not want to have some personal information. If you learn something about a person such as his or her race or that he or she has a disability, the information could be used to claim discrimination if you do not hire the individual, even if the person was not selected for a valid reason. In addition, postings can be placed by people other than the individual. There have been incidents in which young professionals whose friends consider a site purely social post something negative.

With Twitter, a job posting can go "viral," which means it could generate too many responses or even negative comments that you cannot control.

Finally, consider the fact that posting exclusively on social networks may limit reaching out to a diverse group of candidates. It is advisable to use other methods if you are using social media. If you choose to use social networks to post your position, make sure you know how to use then effectively.

Getting Professional Help

If you have tried to recruit candidates on your own and have been less than successful or if you do not have the time, resources, or expertise, you might consider working with a professional recruiting company. These firms recruit and source candidates, screen and interview them, and then present you with individuals who look like potential fits. You still need to interview and make the hiring decision. Larger firms may even have pools of potential candidates they have been in contact with, so the time to hire can be reduced. Often candidates from these firms are what are called "passive" candidates, who are currently employed but who would be willing to change jobs for the right opportunity.

Most professional recruiting firms charge a flat fee based on your projected salary for the first year the candidate would be employed. That rate varies but can typically be between 20 percent and 35 percent. So if you are hiring someone who will be paid $60,000, you would pay the firm $12,000 to $21,000.

Some firms charge a "contract" fee that you pay even if they do not find a candidate whom you hire. These fees usually include a guarantee that the firm will replace someone hired within a certain time period if the candidate voluntarily leaves. Other firms charge a "contingency" fee, meaning they will only charge you if they find someone that you actually hire.

Other companies that focus on lower-level professionals might charge a lower fee but would employ the person for some time period, usually 90 days, during which time the individual would work at your company through a contract with the employment firm. If you decided to make the person a regular employee before the end of the 90-day period, you would likely need to negotiate a settlement or pay out the total fee.

When considering this approach, you should make sure to vet the vendor just as carefully as you would any vendor by asking the following questions:

- What are your statistics on your typical time to hire, and how long do candidates stay at the companies?
- What size companies do you usually work with, and in what industries and geographies have you recruited HR professionals?
- What levels/titles of HR professionals have you recruited?
- Provide us with at least three references from companies that have used your services and that are in our industry.
- How much of your business is in recruiting HR professionals? (Aim for 50 percent or higher as these companies should have good connections in the HR field.)

Like any service contract, you should get a signed agreement with the specific details of the arrangement.

Though these ideas may sound appealing, keep in mind they do not release you from all the time and even money spent in the search. Recruiting firms may find candidates for you and often do check backgrounds or other "vetting," but you will still want to spend time meeting with the agency/firm reps and interviewing candidates.

Document Your Recruiting Plan

Complete Decision Worksheet 4.1 (Recruiting Plan). This document will be used for the activities you will pursue even if you get help with the recruiting process.

Picking the Right Candidate

If you have followed the steps up to this point, you should have a collection of resumes from candidates interested in your HR professional position. If you are lucky, you may have generated plenty of interest.

If not, you need to review your process and determine whether a problem exists and what it is. Some things to consider and change are detailed in Table 4.2.

TABLE 4.2 **CAUSES AND SUGGESTED SOLUTIONS IF TOO FEW OR NOT QUALIFIED CANDIDATES**		
RESULT/PROBLEM	**POSSIBLE CAUSES**	**SOME SOLUTIONS**
Too few resumes/candidates	Competitive job market	Revise your criteria
	Ineffective recruiting methods	•Improve posting •Use additional resources/sites •Use professional recruiter
Resumes/candidates don't meet requirements—over- or underqualified	No candidates with your criteria available	Revise the criteria up or down
Qualified candidates turn down offer	Criteria and pay range don't match	Consider changing pay range or hiring a candidate who has potential and developing him or her

But now what? How do you determine if what you read in the resumes is true, and if the candidate is the one you want?

In the next chapter we will explore how to use a series of filters to select the best available candidate.

DECISION WORKSHEET 4.1. **RECRUITING PLAN**		
Recruiting plan for [job title]		
FACTOR	**DEADLINE**	**INVOLVE**
Establish critical criteria 1. 2. 3.		
Pay range		
Create a posting and include: •Location of job •Positive information about company •General description of the position •Required/desired education and experience •Desired certifications •Information on how to apply, including where to send resume		
Postings/ads Budget: Ads/fees for posting _____ Background check _____ Other _____ Where to post: Websites:		

CONTINUED →

FACTOR	DEADLINE	INVOLVE
Professional organizations:		
Colleges/universities:		
State job service:		
Outplacement firms:		
Newspaper or other media:		
Networking: Personal: Who, where, when Social networks: LinkedIn HR-specific Other:		

CHAPTER 5

The Selection and Hiring Process

The selection process includes reviewing resumes and applications, initial screening, interviewing and using assessments, and performing background and reference checks.

The planning process we have used helps ensure that you know what skills and knowledge your HR professional should have. The other significant piece is the culture of your workplace. Do you have a traditional, predictable workplace, or are you in an industry where the work environment changes rapidly? Do you have a realistic understanding of your culture, not just a picture of what you want it to be? Is the culture you have now what you expect it to be like three to five years from now? Culture includes management styles and values and environment, including the physical surroundings and the expected dress code.

The culture is somewhat driven by and should support the kind of business you have and your market strategy. For example, a high-tech software firm focused on developing the latest product might have a highly flexible culture that encourages creativity and free leadership, whereas a manufacturing environment driven by a focus on on-time delivery might be more structured and rigid, using a chain of command. If you have a structured business focused on cost control, you might have a centralized management structure where control is at the top. In a customer-centered business with multiple locations, management may be decentralized, so your sites can respond to specialized customer and stakeholder needs.

It may be helpful to analyze your culture by selecting where your organization falls within these cultural indicators in Decision Worksheet 5.1 (Culture Analysis).

Being aware of your current culture and how it supports your business is important particularly when hiring an HR professional who can help you keep or change your culture as the manager focusing on the employees.[1] Look at your results, and consider how well the culture supports your current and future business. If you are looking to change your culture, you might want an HR professional who can help you do this. If you want to maintain your culture, looking for someone who can support that is your goal.

Reviewing the case studies from Chapter 2 will give you an idea about how this might work. In Case Study A, the Small Community Bank likely has a more structured culture with a focus on organized schedules and decision control due to the highly regulated nature of its business. The bank needs an HR professional who can cope with this culture. However, given the challenges it faces with recruitment, the bank may want to hire an HR practitioner who can help it become more flexible to attract younger candidates who want flexibility in their workplace.

In Case Study B, the Family-Owned Business may be more middle of the road in terms of culture because manufacturing tends to be somewhat structured, but having multiple locations may mean it is more decentralized. The business' continued success may indicate that it has been able to make changes. Its HR professional needs to be comfortable with this culture and should probably have experience in a similar culture. If the HR professional has worked many years in a more structured environment, he or she may not be happy at the Family-Owned Business.

The Elder Care and Nursing Business in Case Study C might be much more variable due to the services it provides, though it has schedules and regulations to deal with. Every patient/client is different, and the business needs to have a culture that responds to those needs. An HR professional who wants a structured environment may not be a good fit here.

The HR competencies discussed in Chapter 3 give some insight as to the types of people who fit in specific cultures. In this chapter we will focus on how you can find out if candidates fit your current or desired culture. (Using your results in Decision Worksheet 5.1 (Culture Analysis), you can select some interview questions in Decision Worksheet 5.3 (Interview Questions) later in this chapter.) In addition, as you review resumes, you can look for individuals who have experience in similar organizations and industries.

Hiring and Selection Using Filters

The process recommended here is one that is effective for any hiring. We will explore the specific filters with a focus on components that relate to HR. All are important to an effective hire and should be considered to help you make a decision.

Resume Review

The basics of resume review hold true for any position you might hire for. Good resumes are well organized, have no grammar or spelling errors, and do not list unexplained time gaps.

As you review resumes, you want to target the information that you had in your posting and in your job description. If the basic components are in a resume, consider going to the next step with the individual.

Look for industry connections or experience in similar companies. Keep in mind, though, that if you are in banking, for instance, you might be attracted to candidates with HR banking experience, but someone who can bring new experience or ideas to your company might be the better candidate. Similar cultures might be more crucial than the same industry.

Consider what the resume can tell you about the culture the individual may have experience in or be most comfortable with. For example, he or she may have been in heavy industry manufacturing for five years, which could indicate a comfort level with more structured cultures. If your culture is highly variable, ask yourself whether the candidate will be able to cope with it. On the other hand if you are looking to make your culture somewhat more structured, the candidate may be able to bring relevant and appropriate ideas and approaches to you.

Do not limit yourself too much. For example, you may not be in a position to pay for relocation expenses, so you might reject a resume form an individual who has an out-of-state address. If the candidate looks promising otherwise, it may be worth a call as the candidate might be willing or able to pay for a move, or he or she may already be in the process of moving.

From a legal standpoint it is never a good idea to focus on issues that could be discriminatory if they have nothing to do with the requirements of the position. You may incorrectly assume that a person who appears to be older will want too much money or will want to retire soon. In reality that person might be just fine with the pay range and may plan to work for many years. Ignore the candidate, and you might lose a great candidate.

Look for recent education or continuing professional development. In HR it is critical for individuals to be life-long learners because aspects like legal issues change constantly. Membership in professional associations also demonstrates a desire to be current, and the candidate likely has a strong network of professional colleagues. Membership in the Society for Human Resource Management (SHRM), The Association for Talent Development (ATD), and other HR organizations can be beneficial.

Remember that a resume is just the first screen, and given that it is not a signed, legal document like an application form, it might be embellished by the candidate.

Initial Screening

Often the first screen after the resume is a phone call. In the call you want to gather important information by asking some basic questions.

After explaining the essential requirements of the position, including location(s), typical work hours, primary job duties, ask, "Would this position fit what you are looking for?"

Next ask questions related to your priority needs; for example, for an HR position that involves a lot of recruiting, "Tell me about your recruiting experience."

You can also explore questions related to the specific resume information. Keep to job-related questions. These are HR professionals who are well aware of potentially discriminatory questions. If you ask risky questions, they may assume that you have a negative work environment.

This is also a good time to verify that the individual is satisfied with the pay range you can afford by asking, "What kind of pay range would you need?" Often, candidates want to defer this question by asking what the job pays so they can say something within that range. You will get a better idea of what candidates really want if you stay firm and let them know that if they cannot give you an answer, you cannot consider them for the position. Keep in mind that HR professionals, more than most job candidates, probably have some idea about what an HR job should pay.

While engaged in this discussion, you can assess candidates' communication skills. It is critical in the HR field that professionals have strong communication skills. If they do not have the ability to communicate well on the phone, they might not be worth considering.

Decision Worksheet 5.2 (Phone Screen) will help you document the information you gather. For consistency, use the same questions for each candidate.

Face-to-face Interviewing

The next step is the face-to-face interview. Some people assume that HR professionals would be great as interviewees because they have plenty of experience on the other side of the table. This is not necessarily the case. Interviewing is a different skill set. This meeting, particularly when dealing with HR professionals, should be considered a conversation, not an inquisition. You are there to evaluate the candidate, and he or she is there to evaluate you and your organization. It is important to make it a discussion so that the candidate can ask questions, too.

In the beginning you should provide some basic information about your organization and culture and try to help the candidate feel comfortable. You want to see what the candidate is really like, not what he or she is like when nervous!

If you plan on additional rounds of interviews, this first round may involve only you and the candidates. You can include others in the interview, but again, unless the person will be regularly addressing a large group of managers, it is off-putting to have a first interview done by a group; one-on-one is better.

Asking strategic questions and making sure you spend more time listening than talking will help you have an interview where you elicit useful information that will help you select the right person. You should always have a list of questions that you plan to ask all candidates. You can still follow up with questions that expand on their answers or that explore information on the resume that you did not cover in the screen call.

Your questions should include general, broad questions; specific questions related to the technical needs of the job; and some philosophical questions that reveal culture fit. Decision Worksheet 5.3 (Interview Questions) gives you some to choose from. You do not need to limit yourself to these questions, but they will give you some ideas. Keep your specific job and your company culture in mind when you select questions. You may want to choose questions for the first interview as well as the second interview now. They are grouped under categories such as general questions, specific technical areas, and competency questions.

It is best to limit the number of questions to six to eight for a one-hour interview. Ask the same questions of each candidate. If the second interview is planned to be longer, more questions might make sense.

General Interview Thoughts

Effective interviewing also includes adhering to a risk-free process. This means that all interview questions should be job-related. You should not venture into questions that could be considered discriminatory or those that probe into personal or confidential information. Asking these questions of HR professionals increases your risk because they are likely to know what is appropriate to ask and what is not. You should not go further if the person reveals personal information. HR professionals generally would not do this, and doing so may be a red flag about their understanding of appropriate interview practices.

Documenting the interviews is highly recommended. Using a report form like Decision Worksheet 5.4 (Interview Report Form) can help capture your thoughts about each candidate. The form should be completed soon after each interview so that your thoughts will be fresh. Later you can review the information to compare candidates.

The same recommendation for interviewing carries over to documentation: Do not document personal information.

You can use this worksheet after to add the questions you will ask from the Decision Worksheet 5.3 (Interview Questions) to capture the information for each candidate.

Get Others Involved

As you go through the interview process, it might be valuable to involve other managers, particularly those who will be working directly with your HR professional. If the position reports directly to you, you may want the opinion of others, but you may want to make the final hiring decision. If this is the case, make sure you make that clear to anyone else you involve.

When you involve other managers you get their "read" on whether they believe they can work with the candidates. You also gain more buy-in to supporting the person you select when the new employee starts work. This is paramount when it comes to HR professionals because they need to have the cooperation and support of all managers.

You should make sure that other interviewing managers are knowledgeable about standard interview practices, including having developed a list of questions to ask each candidate. Provide them with a copy of Decision Worksheet 5.4 (Interview Report Form) to complete and return to you.

If multiple people will be interviewing, work with them to coordinate their questions. Though you want them to ask different questions, it may be good to have some overlap or even one question that is the same to see if the candidate answers differently to different people.

Second Interviews

When hiring for an HR or any professional role, you should invite the candidates you liked most back for a second interview. It gives you another impression and an opportunity to probe for more depth or have new questions answered. The second interview may be when you get others involved. Even HR professionals are nervous when they are interviewed, and this second chance may give them an opportunity to do a better job interviewing.

As in the first round of interviews, plan questions ahead of time, document the information, and debrief to discuss the results.

By now you should have a final candidate or a smaller pool of candidates to consider through the final filters.

Reference and Background Checking

It is important to do reference checks on all candidates before you make an offer of hire for any hiring situation. Background checks may be particularly vital for an HR professional because even at lower-levels HR professionals deal with information and data that may be highly confidential. Also, HR professionals are expected to help lead ethical behaviors and implement workplace rules, so you want to make sure they have virtually spotless backgrounds and have provided truthful information throughout the recruiting process.

Be aware, however, that various state, local, and even federal regulations may restrict background checking processes to prevent unintentional discrimination by employers. Credit checks for HR professionals may not be considered valid unless you can prove there is a business case for doing them. Minor criminal issues, or those that occurred more than 10 years ago, may not be valid to consider. This is not legal advice, and you should follow your legal counsel's advice and make sure you use background checks appropriately.

How to Perform Effective Reference Checks

Reference checks, if done well, can give you the necessary information to verify what you believe you have seen in the candidate up to this point through the other filters, resume, screening, and interviews. It is recommended that you ask the candidate(s) for the names of and contact information for at least three references. If you obtain conflicting responses from the first two, you have a third who can break the tie.

Individuals whose names the candidate gives you are more likely to be willing to talk to you. Companies in states that do have not laws protecting them from prosecution related to reference information might have policies prohibiting people from giving references.

You may be thinking that references recommended by the candidate would have only positive reviews of the candidate. But, if done well, you can still receive beneficial information from almost any reference. The questions you ask and how you ask them are important. In addition, HR professionals are often the people you will be talking to as references for the HR professional, and they value the good resource for the hiring decision more than any manager. As noted before, if the candidate gives you the reference contacts, the individuals are more likely to be willing to talk to you, and you should not be hesitant to ask them your questions.

You also want to request that at least one of the reference names be for a former manager or supervisor of the candidate; using only co-workers, employees, and customers or vendors will not contribute a management perspective.

What Questions and How to Ask Them

There are several things you want to learn from a reference, including what his or her relationship with the candidate is, the type of work the candidate has done, how well the candidate communicates and performs on the job, the candidate's best traits and weaknesses, and the reference's opinion of the candidate's ability to do the target job.

Decision Worksheet 5.5 (Reference Checking Form) is a guide for your reference calls.

The questions in this worksheet are likely to reduce some helpful information from references. Using reliable questioning techniques and listening skills will help ensure you are getting the information you need.

Listen for consistent tone of voice throughout the discussion. If the person sounds excited and then drops off when you ask if he or she would hire or rehire the individual, this may signal a problem. Be patient and wait for answers. Sometimes it is hard for a reference to reveal a weakness, but given enough time he or she may come up with something.

Other Filters

There a several other filters you can use in determining which HR candidate is right for you, including drug testing and personality or specific skills tests.

Drug Testing

If you regularly use drug tests in your workplace, then you will want to use them with HR job candidates too. As mentioned before, the HR professional is often tasked with applying drug testing and working with managers to discipline employees, so the need for them to have a clean slate is that much more imperative. That said, if you have never done a post-offer, pre-start drug test for any other position, you should talk to legal counsel before starting with this position. Drug tests and physicals (usually not needed as a part of an HR hire) should be done after the offer of hire but before the person starts working as the offer would be withdrawn if the individual failed the drug test.

Personality, Skill, and Aptitude Testing

Personality, skills, and aptitude tests can reveal useful information about candidates to further verify your decisions. First consider if the particular testing tool is appropriate for the position. As with drug tests, if you regularly use some general tests for all hires, you should also use them for your HR professional candidates.

Though the author could not find specific pre-employment assessments currently available for HR professionals, SHRM and other organizations are working on development of these assessments, so they may be available in the future.[2] If you plan to use a personality or aptitude test, research to make sure it is valid (that is, the testing company has verified the results as applying to the position) and reliable (measures what it is supposed to measure). The same is true for skills tests. It is generally safer to purchase versus create tests. Sources for assessments include professional HR associations like SHRM, ATD, and Certified Compensation Professional (CPP), mentioned in previous chapters, which may have or develop tools you can use.

Make sure the test fits the job requirements. For example, if your HR professional will often use Excel to work with spreadsheets, then it is fine to test the candidate on his or her Excel skills.

The Job Offer

Hopefully, after all of your planning, work, and analysis, you are ready to offer the job to your new HR professional. If you have communicated throughout the process, this should be a formality.

Once the person says yes, and you have done any post-offer testing, you should call the candidates who were interviewed and not selected to inform them that the job has been filled. Though a rejection letter or e-mail can be used, trying to personally contact a candidate shows respect for the individual who took the time to come to interview. This type of attention is especially advisable in the HR field—though it shows professionalism and courtesy toward anyone—given that human resources is a well-networked community of professionals. The word gets out about your company, and you want to protect your reputation.

DECISION WORKSHEET 5.1. CULTURE ANALYSIS

PLACE AN "X" TO INDICATE YOUR CURRENT CULTURE

Structured (S)	Mid (M)	Variable (V)
COMMUNICATION		
Explicit: precise, clear, frank		Implicit: understood, implied, unspoken
	S M V	
EVALUATING		
Direct negative feedback		Indirect negative feedback
	S M V	
LEADING		
Chain of command		Unrestricted, democratic, free
	S M V	
DECIDING		
Top down		By consensus, agreement
	S M V	
DISAGREEING		
Confrontational		Avoidance
	S M V	
PERSUADING		
Only those involved		All must agree
	S M V	
SCHEDULING		
Organized, controlled		Flexible, unscheduled
	S M V	
TRUSTING		
Focus on the task		Based on relationships
	S M V	

DECISION WORKSHEET 5.2. **PHONE SCREEN**	
Position title:	
Candidate name:	
Date of prescreen:	
BASIC QUESTIONS	**ANSWERS**
Components of position described:	
How would this location be for you?	
Would these typical work hours be something you could do?	
The basic job duties are:	
Tell me about your experience in those areas.	
Questions specific to the job needs (add written questions here)	

          CONTINUED →

BASIC QUESTIONS (CONTINUED)	ANSWERS (CONTINUED)
Questions specific to the resume information (add written questions here)	
What would your desired compensation/ pay range be?	
Name of screener:	

DECISION WORKSHEET 5.3. INTERVIEW QUESTIONS

GENERAL QUESTIONS

Questions	Answer components to look for	Enter 1 for first interview, 2 for second, etc.
There is a lot of good information on your resume, but tell me something about yourself that you think is important for me to know that I can't see here in writing.	Look for job-, career-, or company-related answers. If candidates launch into some unrelated personal story, they may not be focused on working for you.	
Why are you interested in this position/company?	Listen for indications that they have done research on the job or the company. Today's HR professionals should have good Internet and research skills.	
What is the value of HR in an organization? Why should we have an HR professional position?	Listen for some of the reasons you decided you need an HR professional (see Chapter 1). Answer should also include a view of HR that is similar to yours.	
What do you think would be the biggest challenge for you if you got this job?	Listen for research or how well they listened when you described the job in the phone screen.	
What are the most important qualities and skills that an HR professional should have? Which of these do you excel?[a]	Look for the skills you have identified that you need. (Consider the competencies in Chapter 3.)	

CULTURE

Think back to your experiences at work so far in your career, even considering unpaid work or volunteer jobs, and describe the best work or job you have had so far.	Listen for components of your HR position and the organization's culture.	
Describe your best boss.	Look for similarities to the manager and management style in your company. Answers may tell you if they prefer independence or being managed.	
Is it better to work alone on something or as a part of a team? Why?	Considering your company culture and the position, will the person be expected to work as a part of a team? Best answer explains that it depends on the project.	
What do you do to make your subordinates tell you both, the good news and the bad news, the things they think you want to hear, and the things you need to hear?[a]	Answer reveals management style. If they have good examples of both, they are open and likely not directive.	

    CONTINUED →

CULTURE (CONTINUED)		
Give me examples in previous jobs where you thought you were given too much autonomy and examples where you thought you were given too little.	Listen for examples to reveal if the person prefers to be managed or independent with little management intervention. Match to your culture or not?	
What kinds of pressure do you feel in your job? Tell me about them. How do you deal with them?	Look for how answers relate to the pressures in your organization; consider if the candidate can deal with your pace.	
Which is better, a structured environment or a flexible one?	Answer may show what kind of environment they prefer. Look for the match with current and future culture in your organization. Best answers consider when each environment is better to use given the situation.	
Tell me about a time when you had to deliver bad news to an employee and how you handled it.	Answer may indicate if they are comfortable with providing direct or indirect negative feedback. Are they confrontational, or do they feel uncomfortable with conflict?	
SPECIFIC TECHNICAL: WORKFORCE PLANNING & EMPLOYMENT QUESTIONS		
How do you determine if a candidate is right for the position you are hiring for?	Listen for the processes described in previous chapters: sourcing, selecting, etc.	
Tell me about creative recruiting strategies you have used in your work.	Look for strategies that would relate to your organization's needs.	
What do you think will be the biggest challenge for recruiting for our company in the next five years?	Expect reference to recent data on available employees, retirement issues, etc.	
Tell me about a time when a manager wanted you to terminate an employee in contrast to your company's termination policy. How did you approach the situation? What was the outcome?[a]	Listen for steps taken by candidates to influence the manager to change his/her mind. Also, look for lessons learned about how to handle similar situations particularly if the efforts failed. Look for when, if at all, the problem was kicked up to the manager, and compare with what you'd expect.	
What would be the steps you would take if you were responsible for reducing staff by 10%?[a]	Look for references to legal issues, morale problems, and good strategies. **NOTE**: Using this question could send a signal that the company has layoff plans. You may want to explain, after hearing the response, that you wanted to understand how the candidate would handle a difficult situation but that there are no layoff plans.	

CONTINUED →

SPECIFIC TECHNICAL: BUSINESS MANAGEMENT AND STRATEGY		
Tell me about your networks, including those that you have in HR and those in other business areas.	Listen for current sources and connections that relate to your business.	
If you get this job, you will need to establish relationships with the department managers and supervisors. How would you go about doing this?	Answer should include meeting with individuals to understand their perspectives as well as listening to how HR can help them.	
Describe your understanding of strategic and business planning.	Good answers include the aspects of risk and opportunity analysis, looking at internal and external factors that affect business, and possibly examples of how they participated in strategic planning in past jobs.	
Tell me about your budgeting experience. What amounts of money have you been responsible for in past jobs?	Answer should include budget ranges similar to yours. Responsibilities could include planning, projecting, managing spending, etc.	
What can you tell me about how laws and regulations are established, and what do you think is coming down the legislative pipeline that will affect the employment relationship?	Listen for awareness of trends in legislation and a basic understanding of the difference in federal and state laws and regulatory and enforcement bodies.	
How would you as an HR professional make sure that employees know about our business values?	Answer should include communicating information using methods the employees will understand as well as including values as drivers of policies, processes, etc.	
If I spoke to former managers that you dealt with as the HR professional, what would they say about you?	Listen for respect and even challenges they overcame.	
How do you keep yourself up-to-date on legal and HR trends?	May include membership in professional organizations and reading websites, publications, etc.	
What was the most recent HR-related book you read, and what did you think of the information presented in it?	Answer may include business books. It is important that specifics be discussed, not just general comments about the book.	

CONTINUED →

SPECIFIC TECHNICAL: COMPENSATION AND BENEFITS		
Tell me about a workers' compensation situation you've managed where the employee was not able to return to work for more than three months after the injury.[a]	Listen for details related to your organization and direct involvement in investigations, employee communication, and knowledge of workers' compensation.	
What would you do if faced with creating cost-cutting measures for benefits premiums?[a]	Look for experience versus just knowledge.	
Have you processed payroll? What other payroll functions are you familiar with?	Listen for information related to your organization's process, vendor, etc.	
Tell me about a pay or benefits problem you had to resolve. What was the outcome, and what might you do differently if you had to face the same problem again?	Look for process, investigation technique, learning from mistakes.	
What has your current company (or most recent employer) done in response to the PPACA?[a]	The PPACA is the Patient Protection and Affordable Care Act—often called Obamacare. Listen for benefits knowledge and direct involvement as it relates to your organization.	
SPECIFIC TECHNICAL: EMPLOYEE AND LABOR RELATIONS		
Have you ever worked in a union environment? *Yes*: What were the positives/ negatives? *No*: What steps would you take to prevent a union?	*Yes*: If the relationship with the union and employees is good, some things like discipline can be somewhat easier to implement at times, but it puts a barrier between the company and the employees and can cause more expense. *No*: Open communication, ensuring fair/consistent treatment of employees, good supervisors/ managers, a climate of respect for all.	

CONTINUED →

SPECIFIC TECHNICAL: EMPLOYEE AND LABOR RELATIONS (CONTINUED)		
Describe to me in a few sentences the purpose of the following basic federal regulations (select one or more, as applicable): • Title VII/Civil Rights Act • FLSA • FMLA • ADAa	• Title VII/Civil Rights Act: Protects against job discrimination based on race, color, religion, gender, or national origin. Where sexual harassment claims are based. • FLSA (Fair Labor Standards Act): Sets minimum wage, overtime, child labor, and other wage standards. • FMLA (Family and Medical Leave Act): Requires some employers to provide employees with unpaid leave for birth or placement for adoption of child, for one's own serious health condition, or for the serious health condition of spouse, child, or parent. Expended to provide leave for families of military under certain circumstances. • ADA (Americans with Disabilities Act): Protects qualified persons with disabilities against job discrimination.	
What state laws in _____ have you had to deal with in your HR work?	Expect specific information on states in which the individual has done HR work. If they know the laws of the state that your business is in, that is better. If they don't know your state laws, ask how they would educate themselves, and expect answers with reference to reputable resources, SHRM, legal counsel, etc.	
Tell me about your knowledge of/ involvement with progressive discipline.[a]	Listen for direct involvement with the process as well as coaching of managers/supervisor. Progressive discipline is an approach where steps of discipline are applied based on the seriousness or repetition of negative behaviors. Usually includes employee counseling, verbal warning, written warning, suspension with or without pay, corrective action agreement, and termination.	
Describe your knowledge of or involvement with performance evaluation processes.	Look for the type of program used, frequency of performance reviews (should be at least annually), and recognition of possible legal issues as well as the need to have regular communication with employees, not just once a year.	

CONTINUED →

SPECIFIC TECHNICAL: EMPLOYEE AND LABOR RELATIONS (CONTINUED)		
An employee tells you about a sexual harassment allegation but then tells you he or she doesn't want to do anything about it; he/she just thought you should know. How do you respond?[a]	Answer should include telling the employee that by law the HR professional must do something about the complaint. Assure the employee that human resources will do its best to be as confidential as possible. Ask the employee about the situation, witnesses, etc. Document the conversation, and seek legal advice. Encourage the employee to tell the perpetrator to stop the behavior. Candidates shouldn't assume that what they were told is the whole truth.	
Tell me about work you have done with labor law attorneys in your HR experience. If you can, give me some examples of the types of issues you dealt with.	They should not reveal anything specific, including names of companies, employees, etc. Should talk about what their role was with counsel, if they worked back and forth or just handed things over without involvement in the resolution of the issue.	
Give me an example of one of the most difficult employee relations problems you had to deal with. What did you do, and what was the outcome?	Listen for the level of problem and the complexity. The HR professional should have done an investigation and should refer to any legal implications.	
Tell me about your policy development experiences. What employment policies have you developed or revised? What is your experience in compiling or revising an employee handbook?[a]	Look for the extent of experience, direct involvement, and also education of employees and managers on the policies once developed.	
SPECIFIC TECHNICAL: EMPLOYEE DEVELOPMENT		
What kind of experience do you have with training employees and managers? What were the training topics? Do you like training? Why?[a]	Listen for related experiences and topics. Look for more than a simple reason they like it (they are likely to say yes). Something like, "Training is critical if employees/managers are to be able to do their jobs," or "Training demonstrates a good faith effort if there are legal issues."	
Tell me about any training or development programs you have developed, whom they were for, where you got the content, and who delivered the training?	Look for related needs and understanding of the need to customize training to the audience.	

CONTINUED →

SPECIFIC TECHNICAL: EMPLOYEE DEVELOPMENT (CONTINUED)		
How do you evaluate the effectiveness of an employee training program?	Reaction: Did employees like it? Learning: Tests, before and after or after. Behavior: Performance on the job. Results: Have business conditions improved, better productivity, improved income/profit?	
What criteria do you use when determining training plans and budgeting for training and development?	Answer should include determine who needs training; make sure the problem is truly training rather than a lack of support or tools, etc.; determine the best methods against the cost; set measurable goals.	
What do you see as the greatest challenges for training at this company in the next few years?	Listen for comments related to knowledge of your organization or industry as well as retirement of Baby Boomers, skills gaps, etc.	
What methods can be used in addition to training classes to develop employees?	Examples should include coaching, on-the-job training, mentoring, cross-training, job shadowing, job rotation, stretch assignments, and tuition reimbursement.	
SPECIFIC TECHNICAL: RISK MANAGEMENT		
HR professionals often deal with legal and ethical situations. Tell me about an ethical situation you have encountered and the part you took in resolving it.[a]	Look for how the situation might relate to your organization. Answer should include efforts made to create or enforce company policies. Answer should recommend considering the level of issue described and working with managers and legal counsel if appropriate.	
Tell me about a workplace injury you had to investigate and how you handled it.	Listen for process and references to legal issues.	
Give me an example of a time you had to deal with a workplace safety issue.	Look for specific involvement and steps taken.	
What do you know about OSHA and how it applies to our organization?	Listen for understanding of your organization and OSHA law.	
How would you deal with a health crises in the workplace?	Answer should include methods of instruction for health safety in your workplace and purchase of equipment as well as contingency plans for work continuation.	

CONTINUED →

SPECIFIC TECHNICAL: RISK MANAGEMENT (CONTINUED)		
What are the components of an emergency response program for the workplace?[a]	•Preparedness: First, prepare to protect yourself, others, and items of great importance in the event an emergency/disaster occurs. Train employees on how to respond, and assign key employees to be responsible for aspects. •Response: When there is an actual occurrence, administer first aid or get medical attention for victims if necessary. Attend to other emergency procedures that must take place to lessen the impact. •Recovery: After things are under control, begin the clean up or repair any damage, and if necessary, call in professional restoration services; determine how the business will continue or restart. •Mitigation: Ask how this disaster, accident, or emergency happened and how any problems that occurred in handling the incident be lessened.	
COMPETENCY QUESTIONS		
HR expertise		
How do you stay current on changes in labor laws and regulations?	Listen for recent legal training/ education or development program attendance; membership and participation in related HR organizations; references to reading books, websites, HR blogs, etc.	
Tell me what you know about our company/business.	Expect detail based on what might be available via websites or contacts. Reference to similar businesses is good too.	
If you got this position, what would be your biggest challenge as far as learning the business?	Answer should include recognition of areas of lack of experience or knowledge.	
What have you done in the last two years to keep up-to-date with changes in the HR field?	Listen for recent HR training/ education or development program attendance; membership and participation in related HR organizations; references to reading books, websites, HR blogs, etc.	

CONTINUED →

Relationship management

If I asked the managers and employees at your past positions about you, what would they say?	Answer should include specific information about how they came to the person for help and collaboration. Great answer would include a time when they won a manager or employee over who was skeptical.	
How would you make yourself a part of our management team, if you got this job?[a]	Listen for a plan to meet with and listen to the needs of the managers and offer of "how can I help" type questions.	
Describe your professional network and how you maintain it.	Expect to hear about a large network of professionals from human resources and the industry as well as outside both. Good answer would include regular efforts to reach out and grow the network.	
What is HR's role in an organization? Why is it important?	Answer should include reference to how HR should understand the business and contribute to it from the HR perspective. Might include recognition that an HR professional must always maintain a balanced focus on the organization and the employees alike.	
What does customer service mean in HR?	Listen for an understanding that HR needs to serve both management and employees by helping each understand the other to support the organization.	

Consultation

Give me an example of a workforce issue you solved.	Listen for the level or difficulty of the problem and the application of HR knowledge.	
Tell me about a time you provided HR expertise to help solve a company problem.[a]	Look for recognition from other managers and employees that the person is an expert in HR.	
What do you think the phrase "creative problem-solver" means in HR?	Answer should include a perspective that includes inviting ideas from others, not just being "rule" oriented, etc.	

CONTINUED →

Leadership and navigation

Tell me about a time when you used collaboration to solve a problem.	Expect a workplace problem that included listening, engaging others, and flexibility.
When should you use consensus decision-making versus voting or directing in HR?	Answer should include an acknowledgement that at times due to business needs or legal restrictions you need to make a directive decision but that consensus is often better because all agree to accept the decision.
How have you considered you company's culture when participating in a new project or program?	Listen for an example that clearly shows an understanding of the business and the value of selling an idea or moving something forward using that idea.
Tell me about a time when you participated in a company-wide initiative. What was your role?[a]	Look for leadership roles and understanding of the business and culture.
Give me an example of when you were responsible for an unpopular change and how you approached it.[a]	Answer should include reference to determining why it was unpopular as well as efforts to engage the people who were dealing with the change in making some decisions.

Communication

At one time or another, we have all had some problems getting our point across when talking with another person (directly or on the telephone). Give me some examples of when this may have happened to you.	Answer should include a focus on listening to the other person, determining what motivates the other person, and then asking clarifying questions. May include waiting for the person to calm down if he or she is upset.
What different approaches do you use in talking with different people? (How do you know you are getting your point across?)	Listen for an understanding that people differ in understanding based on intellect, original language, life experience, education, etc.
Tell me about a time you had to coach a manager who was having a problem with an employee. What happened?	Best answer should be a serious situation with positive results. Examples of less success with some "learning" are also good.
Describe a time when you used your listening skills to "sell" an idea to your boss.	Example is best if it shows an understanding of the boss' perspective and motivations as well as the culture and business needs.
HR professionals need to keep good documentation. What does this mean?	Listen for a focus on clear and concise written communication as well as detailed information to protect the company from legal risks.

CONTINUED →

Diversity and inclusion		
What does "diversity" mean?	Answer should include the realization that diversity is not just race or gender but that everyone is diverse as all individuals are different in some way.	
Tell me about a time that you had to help an employee who was "different" become a part of a team.[a]	Listen for efforts to educate employees about the value of differences or different thinking.	
Describe a time when others disagreed with you. What did you do?	Look for a willingness to listen and change based on input from others.	
What do you see as the most challenging aspect of a diverse working environment? What steps have you taken in the past to meet this challenge?[a]	Listen for an understanding of diversity and direct involvement in dealing with diversity problems.	
What was/is the diversity value at your current/former employer? What impact did you make on this value?[a]	Listen to hear if the past/current environment is like the one at your company. Listen for candidates' feelings about the diversity environment and how they improved the situation.	
Ethical practice		
Describe for me a time when you have come across questionable business practices. How did you handle the situation?[a]	Listen for efforts to resolve the problem by investigating confidentially, working with legal counsel, and working with managers.	
Have you ever faced a significant ethical problem at work? How did you handle it?	Look for HR and legal knowledge and aspects like efforts to resolve the problem by investigating confidentially, working with legal counsel, and working with managers.	
Describe a time when you made a mistake at work. How did you deal with this situation, and what was the outcome?	Seriousness of the mistake is important as well as self-acceptance and learning going forward.	
Have you worked in a situation where an employee, vendor, or supplier had a conflict of interest? How did you handle this?[a]	Look for understanding of values within the particular industry and including them with the problem resolutions as well as educating others about reducing business risk.	
Explain the phrase "work ethic." How would you describe your work ethic?	Answer should include a dedication to being honest. Listen for a balanced view on dedication to the job and a personal life.	

CONTINUED →

Critical evaluation

What was one of the toughest problems you ever solved? What process did you go through to solve it?	Consider the depth of the answer, and look for a step-by-step approach using critical thinking and research.	
How do you analyze different options to determine which is the best alternative?	Answer should include analysis of each alternative, research, working with others.	
Describe for me how your prior positions required you to be proficient in the analysis of technical reports?	Determine if the type of reports is similar to the kind you use.	
How have you approached solving a problem that initially seemed insurmountable?	Look for the business importance of the problem and a logical approach to the resolution as well as collaborating with managers.	
Where do you go to research a decision?[a]	Answer may include professional organizations, experts, managers, employees who do the job, the Internet, professional publications. Look for multiple sources, not just one.	

Business acumen

Tell me about a time you used your knowledge of the organization to get an idea approved.[a]	Answer should include information on how the knowledge was acquired and negotiating abilities.	
Tell me about a time you used financial, industry, and economic environment data to support a successful project.[a]	Look for a true understanding of financial and economic data, not just popular terms.	
What have you done in your positions at other companies that made a difference to the business and for which you believe you will be remembered?[a]	Answer is best if the action saved the organization in terms of money or time or helped make money.	
What difference does it make to organize departments in a centralized versus decentralized way? Do you have a preference?[a]	Consider your structure. Centralized would be when decisions are made from the top and there are lots of controls. Decentralized departments are those that are given a lot of latitude to make decisions based on their needs, goals. A company that wants to control costs might be more centralized. A creative customer responsive company less so.	
What role does a "corporate culture" play in the success of a company?[a]	Expect a recognition that the culture needs to support the business mission and goals.	

a "Interview Questions: Human Resources Capacity," SHRM Online, http://www.shrm.org/TemplatesTools/Samples/InterviewQuestions/Pages/HumanResourcesCapacity.aspx.

Looking to Hire an HR Leader?

DECISION WORKSHEET 5.4. **INTERVIEW REPORT FORM**	
Job title:	
Candidate name:	
Date:	
Education and experience •Degree/diploma •_____ years' experience in _____ •Other	
Job skills Questions and candidate answers: 1. 2. 3. 4. 5. 6. 7. 8.	

CONTINUED →

Competencies Questions and candidate answers 1. 2. 3. 4.	
Other	
Indicators of success	Indicators of success
Recommendation: ___Consider for hire ___No interest ___Not this position, consider for:	
Interviewer signature_____	

DECISION WORKSHEET 5.5. **REFERENCE CHECKING FORM**	
Job title	
Date	
Name of candidate	
Name of caller	
Name of reference	
Contact phone number	
Company name from candidate	
	Verified: Yes or No (circle)
Relationship provided by candidate	
	Verified: Yes or No (circle)
How do you know [candidate's name]?	
For how long have you known [candidate's name]?	
Please describe the job/ work that the candidate is doing/did.	

CONTINUED →

Tell me about [candidate's name]'s interpersonal communication skills when communicating with [his/her] boss, direct reports, and employees in general, customers, etc.	
How would you rate [candidate's name]'s HR performance on a 1 to 10 scale with 1 being low and 10 high, and why would you give the candidate that rating?	

CONTINUED →

What is the [candidate's name]'s best trait and greatest strength in HR work?	
No one is perfect, so what is a weakness you are aware of when it comes to [candidate's name]'s work?	
(Describe the position briefly.) Do you think [candidate's name] could do this HR job? Why?	
If you had an HR position that reported to you that required [candidate's name]'s skills, would you hire/rehire [her/him]?	Yes: ___ No: ___ Vague, hesitant, unresponsive: ____

CHAPTER
6

Onboarding Your HR Professional

So you have a new HR professional. Now what? The planning does not stop yet. You need to consider what you should have ready before the first day. Though this is a meaningful step for any new employee and you might have an established orientation process, you will want to take some special steps for your HR professional because this individual needs to be able to balance the organization's needs and goals with those of the employees to be effective. The HR professional must be introduced to managers and employees in a way that will set up the new recruit to do the best job for you. Giving your HR professional a solid start will reduce the chance he or she will leave the organization. When you consider the amount of time and resources spent in the recruiting and hiring process, you do not want to have the person walk away.

Understanding the Business

As with any other hire, you should have a process for onboarding your HR professional. Your first step is to make sure that the new HR professional understands your business. If you have an orientation process, he or she should go through it. If not, you need to provide the individual with the appropriate forms to complete: W-4, I-9, etc. Also give the individual copies of any HR policies you have and the employee handbook.

Next you should spend some time with the HR professional to help him or her understand the company's business operations, market strategy, strategic plan, financial data, organizational structure (including the organizational chart), culture, and any other aspects important to your business. You might wonder why the new employee needs this information; after all he or she is doing human resources, not these other things. Keep in mind that the HR function supports all of these other areas. Your HR professional needs to understand the business if she or he is to establish, implement, manage, and assess HR functions that lead to success in these areas.

The depth of information that you provide the HR professional at this point will depend on the level that you have established for the position in the organization. For a more entry-level professional, you may provide a more broad-brush approach. But for the HR manager or higher who will be advising other managers in the organization, you should go deeper.

This introduction to the business may take several meetings and include exposure or tours of your facilities, so the employee can see the work being done; also provide materials the individual can read.

Understanding the Business Leadership

Once the HR professional has some understanding of the business, you need to help him or her understand your expectations. As the owner or leader of the business, you need to help your HR professional know your management philosophy. For example, what are your human resources/people management priorities? What tasks do you expect the HR professional to accomplish? And what are the deadlines?

It might be valuable at this point to give the new hire some organization history and an understanding of your goals for the future.

Encourage the HR professional to communicate with you on a regular basis and to ask questions if he or she needs information or has concerns. Establishing a strong and open communication with your HR professional will pay off as he or she will have a much better chance to support your work and organization. It may be wise in the first 30 days to establish a regular meeting time each day or each week, depending on the level of support your HR professional might need. More entry-level individuals or those who are new to your industry might need more frequent communication.

Getting to Know Managers

Prior to the first day, you should give your managers information on the individual you hired and some understanding of the position's responsibilities. If you have involved the managers in any of the interview process, you may have already done this.

If you expect the HR professional to be successful in shaping and managing your HR functions, you also need to help the other managers understand what you expect from them in terms of cooperation. You should make clear that the HR professional reports to you and that you expect the other managers to recognize whatever authority you are delegating to the new employee.

It is a good idea to plan a group meeting with managers to formally introduce the new HR professional if possible. In addition, you should set up individual meetings with the HR professional and senior managers. By doing this you are establishing the role and responsibilities, and your HR professional is more likely to get cooperation from your managers.

Meeting the Employees

Introducing the HR professional to the employees can take many forms. If you have regular organization-wide meetings, you can include an introduction there. Company newsletters or intranets or e-mail blast introductions can be used. The higher the level of the HR professional the more robust the announcement; for example, an HR coordinator could be introduced by the passive means of e-mail but a director or higher probably should be announced to a meeting of the entire organization (in additional to the more routine methods). Consider how your employees regularly communicate, and use those methods.

Explain to employees what the HR professional is responsible for and how employees can and should communicate with him or her.

Assignments for HR

Once you have educated your HR professional about the company, your philosophy, and the managers and employees, encourage him or her to continue this process. The individual should be expected to set up meetings with key stakeholders like the managers, supervisors, and, perhaps, the top talent, and to attend group or departmental meetings to meet employees.

Coaching the HR professional on the components to be included in the stakeholder meetings is a good idea. First, advise the individual to ask them what human resources can do for them. Second, the HR professional should ask for an understanding of each stakeholder's work or function. Third, the HR professional should share with the stakeholders his or her background or experience.

You may also provide your insights about each of the stakeholder's communication styles to assist the HR professional in starting a collaborative and productive relationship.

Checking Back: 30-60-90-120 Days

The onboarding process does not end with the first day or week. It is critical to check back with the HR professional (not to mention all your senior leadership and top talent) on a regular basis. Plan to meet and discuss learning and progress every 30 days. Ask the HR professional how things are going, if managers and employees are cooperating with him or her, and so on. Even if you have encouraged the HR professional to communicate and ask questions, these planned meetings may provide you with useful data points.

Onboarding Checklist

Decision Worksheet 6.1 (Onboarding Plan) will help you plan your HR professional's orientation, ensuring the new employee is off to a good start. You should probably have this worksheet completed before you start interviewing candidates, as the good ones may ask you about it.

DECISION WORKSHEET 6.1. **ONBOARDING PLAN**

Onboarding plan for _____

ACTIVITY	DATE	NOTES	CHECK IF COMPLETED
First-day paperwork			
Tour of facilities			
Business information: ___ Operations ___ Market strategy ___ Culture ___ Strategic plan ___ Financials ___ Structure ___ Other			
Reporting manager information plan: ___ History ___ Future plans/goals ___ Management style ___ HR priorities/goals ___ Meeting schedule ___ Other items/concerns			
Manager introductions ___ Managers informed about HR ___ Meetings scheduled for introductions ___ Other			

CONTINUED →

ACTIVITY	DATE	NOTES	CHECK IF COMPLETED
Employee announcements ___ Newsletter ___ Intranet ___ E-mail ___ Meetings ___ Other			
Plan for individual manager and HR meetings set.			
Dates set for follow-up meetings: ___ 30 days ___ 60 days ___ 90 days ___ 120 days			

Managing Your HR Professional

In any healthy employment relationship, ongoing feedback is essential. You should have some mechanism for reviewing the performance of your employees, and hopefully your HR professional will help you improve this process.

Your review process should involve regular feedback as well as scheduled formal meetings to discuss performance against established goals. Traditionally, a performance management program includes at least an annual formal review meeting.

HR Performance Goals

One of the keys to a successful performance review is establishing strong performance goals. These goals should be reasonable, focused on supporting the organization and its business plans, and include some measurable component (that is, SMART goals—specific, measurable, achievable, realistic, and time-bound).

The number of goals should be somewhere between five and seven total. Keep in mind that the goals should be to focus the individual on new or significant areas; they do not need to include every task of the job. Based on the performance of the individual and the business plans, the goals are likely to change each year.

Examples of performance goals related to functional areas are listed in Decision Worksheet 7.1 (HR Performance Goals), but yours should be specific to you and your organization.

Continuing Professional Development

Your HR professional should maintain and grow in his or her knowledge to continue to provide you with the best HR services. A number of professional development options exist, and your support for these efforts (that is, budgeting for it) is an investment in your business going forward. In human resources the changes in technology, practices, laws, and regulations may be even more frequent than in other aspects of your business, so keeping up with them is critical.

In addition, education/workshops in project management, business finance, risk management, auditing, and other professional business areas are valuable for your HR professional so he or she can support all aspects of your business. This kind of development may make the HR professional more promotable outside the HR function as your organization grows. What better person to move into other management positions than one who truly understands how to manage employees!

Membership in Professional Organizations

By maintaining membership in professional organizations that do research and that provide educational and networking opportunities, your HR professional will stay aware of changes so that the individual can respond effectively in the position.

Organizations like the Society for Human Resource Management (SHRM) and affiliated local chapters provide resources that include the HR generalist areas. Often the information on the organization's website is a quick way for your HR professional to find answers to HR questions that arise in your workplace. Free or discounted workshops and training programs may also be available.

Some professional organizations focus on support for specific HR functional areas that may be beneficial depending on the responsibilities and challenges faced in your HR function. They include the following:
- Society for Human Resource Management (SHRM) (national/local)
- HR People & Strategy (HRPS)
- Association for Talent Development (ATD)
- WorldatWork
- International Society of Certified Employee Benefit Specialists (ISCEBS)

There are professional organizations and associations that focus on your industry and this can help keep your HR professional knowledgeable about competitive companies, industry trends, top talent, etc.

Professional Certifications

Chapter 4 discussed professional certifications as a way to determine the knowledge of an HR professional. If your HR professional came to you with a particular certification, it may be necessary for him or her to obtain continuing education to maintain that certification. For example, the Professional in Human Resources (PHR) certification offered by the HR Certification Institute (HRCI) is good for three years, but requires the individual to accrue 60 recertification credits in that time span. Other certifications have similar requirements.

If you want your HR professional to support your organization, it is wise to encourage this education and if possible to provide time off and financial reimbursement for classes and workshops. The learning can usually be targeted to what you need in your HR functions, so it becomes a win-win for you and the employee.

If your HR professional does not yet have a certification or wishes to try for a higher level, such as the Senior Professional in Human Resources (SPHR), you might want to support that education.

Other certifications that might prove beneficial are the following:

- Society for Human Resource Management–Certified Professional (SHRM-CP)
- Society for Human Resource Management–Senior Certified Professional (SHRM-SCP)
- Certified Compensation Professional (CCP)
- Certified Professional in Human Resources and Compensation (CPHRC)
- Certified Professional in Learning and Performance Certification (CPLP)
- Global Professional in Human Resources (GPHR)
- Human Resource Business Professional (HRBP)
- Human Resource Management Professional (HRMP)
- Certified Employee Benefit Specialist (CEBS)
- Compensation Management Specialist (CMS)

Formal Education

Because your HR professional needs to work with other managers and needs to understand aspects of your business beyond HR, the individual may be interested in pursuing formal education or a more advanced degree.

If the HR professional has an associate degree in business, for example, he or she may want to complete a bachelor's degree in human resources. If the HR professional already has a bachelor's degree in human resources, maybe acquiring an MBA would make sense for your organization. Some HR professionals even study law given that legal issues comprise a substantial part of human resources.

If supporting this kind of continuing education for your HR professional seems beneficial for your company, it may be a wise investment in the future. HR professionals often make talented operations or financial managers if they have an interest and aptitude in those areas.

Even if the individual does leave your organization someday, while the HR professional is attending classes, he or she is hopefully contributing more to your organization.

Other Ways to Develop Your HR Professional

Though formal approaches to education outside the workplace can help your HR professional grow and contribute, you can also develop the individual by setting up internal opportunities.

Making your HR professional a regular part of your management team, if the position is at or near that level, will help the employee learn more about how the organization operates. The HR professional can also provide input in management decisions from the HR view. For example, if you are considering increasing sales by adding a new product or service, the HR professional will be able to ask questions about what type of employees are needed to do this new work and if the HR professional has good external networks they may have access to information on available talent and insights on people management trends.

Assigning your HR professional to a task group working to solve an organizational problem can have learning benefits for the individual as he or she interacts with other parts of the business and with other managers. Also, the HR professional can bring a different perspective to the issue than the sales or operations manager.

Moreover, having the HR professional work for some time period in another department will help him or her understand the work so that the individual can better assist the manager and employees in that department.

Giving increasing responsibility to the HR professional by adding appropriate reporting relationships can also help the individual grow. An example here might be having the receptionist or the safety manager or plant scheduler report to or share a reporting relationship with human resources.

Ask Your HR Professional

Making development decisions for your HR professional should not be done in isolation. You should encourage each member of your business leadership— which the HR professional may be included—to have an ongoing communication with you about his or her interests.

DECISION WORKSHEET 7.1. **HR PERFORMANCE GOALS**		
FUNCTIONAL AREA	**POSSIBLE GOAL**	**CHECK IF USING**
Business management and strategy	Contribute to the strategic plan in _____.	
	Establish external business contacts to research industry trends related to HR.	
	Create an HR strategic plan that aligns with the company plan.	
	Establish and manage the HR budget reducing expenses by ____% for _____.	
Workforce planning and employment	Reduce the turnover rate by ___ % by implementing more effective recruiting processes.	
	Establish and implement a sourcing and hiring process working with the organization manager by the end of the fiscal year.	
	Train all managers and supervisors on effective and legal interviewing skills by _____.	
	Improve the current record-keeping process for hiring and recruitment.	
	Work with the executive management team to develop a succession and replacement plan for the next five years.	
Total rewards — including pay and benefits	Improve the ratio of pay to sales and profit by devising a new compensation strategy by the end of the fiscal year.	
	Reduce spending on employee benefits by ___ % for the next three years.	
	Increase employee participation in the 401(k) plan by _____.	
	Working with the management team, devise a benefits strategy to improve the services while holding costs steady.	
	Review the current pay structure, and work to make sure it is equitable and meets government requirements to reduce company risk.	
	Research and engage a payroll processing vendor, staying within the established budget goals.	
	Establish an employee wellness program to reduce lost work time.	

CONTINUED →

FUNCTIONAL AREA	POSSIBLE GOAL	CHECK IF USING
Employee and labor relations	Develop strategies that will improve attendance by ___%.	
	Negotiate a labor contract this year that saves the organization ___%.	
	Create and implement a new employee handbook, and roll it out to employees by _____.	
	Educate supervisors about union avoidance techniques.	
	Implement an employee satisfaction survey this year.	
	Reduce unemployment compensation costs by more; follow up on denials and attendance at hearings.	
Employee development	Increase the number of training opportunities for employees while holding down costs.	
	Update OSHA training programs to make them consistent with new regulations.	
	Create a management development program to support succession planning in the next five years.	
	Evaluate the training needs for the _____ employees for the next two years.	
	Establish and implement a harassment prevention training program for _____, including finding an appropriate supplier and scheduling classes for all employees.	
Health, security, and safety	Reduce the number of lost work hours due to injuries by working with production managers and the workers' comp insurance provider.	
	Establish and implement a new facility security policy.	
	Create an emergency response plan by _____.	
	Create a job description and hire a security guard for the facility by _____.	
	Establish a safe work awards program to encourage safety practices within the established budget.	

CHAPTER 8

Should You Outsource Some Aspects of HR?

You may be thinking that the process of hiring an HR professional is time-consuming, and you are right. However, keep in mind that spending the time to do the task well (hiring a top-performing HR professional) is an investment in your organization's future.

As you worked your way through the decision worksheets in Chapter 2, you should have realized that an onsite, dedicated professional who knows your business is likely a much better decision than hiring an outside organization to manage your most significant resources—your employees.

That said, there may be times when considering outsourced help might be more efficient, save you money, or free your HR professional to engage in more strategic efforts that add greater value to the organization. Most businesses use attorneys to assist and represent them when faced with, for example, Equal Employment Opportunity Commission (EEOC) or workers' compensation issues. In these cases, companies need experts for a period of time, so hiring a full-time, in-house counsel would not make sense.

Another example might be administrative assistance. If you are expecting significant turnover from retirements in the next three years, you may not want your HR professional to spend too much time entering data and researching the latest tax laws to advise employees on retirement benefits.

Rather, you would no doubt want the HR professional to be working with your management team to come up with strategies for hiring and training new employees, proactively developing key succession plans, reducing company costs associated with retirement, and devising ways to keep some of the soon-to-be-retired employees on the payroll to share their know-how gained over years of experience.

It is wise to hire your HR professional *before* considering outsourcing because he or she should be involved in the selection and management of the vendor. Plus, you may think you cannot find someone who can handle a particular task or function but be surprised by finding just that person.

Other solutions to the retirement example above may include hiring a temporary HR assistant or cross-training and using other company staff to manage a particular project or challenge.

In this chapter we will identify outsourcing solutions for businesses and tactics for vendor selection and management of the outsourcing relationship.

Background

Some HR functions are more suitable for outsourcing than others. Even when you use a vendor to help with these functions, the company and your HR professional must provide information and oversee the work results. Those that are commonly (but not always) outsourced are provided below.[1]

Pay

The compensation functions commonly outsourced are payroll, job evaluation systems, salary surveys, executive compensation design, and expatriate compensation. Outsourcing to third-party administrators for payroll and related tax duties may help you meet filing deadlines and deposit requirements. The reasons for outsourcing may include cost savings, a need to improve customer service, the ability to take advantage of technology not available in-house, or a desire for the HR department to be focused on a more strategic approach within the organization.

Benefits Administration

With the advent of the Affordable Care Act, there may be a trend to providing a defined contribution toward employee health benefits rather than health plans. This may change the climate of health care benefits in the future. Partnering with a third-party benefits administration provider—a practice known as benefits administration outsourcing—can save time while keeping employees happy with the service. Through negotiated contracts, volume buying, and economies of scale, providers can deliver program advantages that individual HR professionals could not secure on their own. Providers can also be enlisted to manage the most challenging part of benefits administration: the annual enrollment process.

Workforce Administration

Workforce administration, an emerging trend in human capital management, refers to the following set of HR functions and activities:
- Development, maintenance, and operation of HR information systems.
- Employee and manager policy and procedure support.
- Employee and manager self-service and customer service.
- Employee data management and records retention.

External Recruitment

Success in outsourcing external recruitment depends on having an effective talent-sourcing strategy, establishing clear performance expectations and measures, and carefully selecting a recruitment partner. The potential benefits include building a strategic recruitment partnership focused on obtaining top-quality talent critical for your success.

Relocation

The need to deal with the unexpected is one reason to outsource various relocation functions. These include claims assistance, audit and payment of invoices, shipment monitoring, expense tracking, reimbursement, and supplementary services.

Employee Rewards and Recognition

Recognition programs can provide incentives and reinforcement for desired employee behaviors in areas such as productivity, sales, workplace safety, years of service, and cooperation with peers. But the programs can be time-consuming to administer. Even a program that simply recognizes employees for years of service involves several tasks for obtaining rewards for the program, such as plaques, certificates, or gifts. Administrative tasks increase as the program becomes more complex and specialized. Outside vendors can be enlisted to handle many of the routine tasks of rewards programs.

Types of HR Outsourcing Options

Application Service Providers

Companies known as application service providers (ASP) remotely host software applications and provide access to and use of the applications over the Internet. Typically, the employer pays these providers a service fee based on use, such as an amount per user per month. The software is designed to help HR professionals offer more transactional-related services to employees without the need of a larger HR team. ASPs typically shift organizations from paper-based file systems to streamlined online systems designed to offer employees self-service. Services offered by ASPs include allowing employees to sign-up for benefits online and to make changes to their accounts, thereby reducing routine intervention of the HR professional, the company, or they may also provide employee access to online training programs.

The pros of using ASPs are time savings for the company and human resources and moving to a paper-free environment. The cons are often the initial as well as ongoing costs. Once the employer starts using the systems, there may be costs for software and system upgrades. There may also be risks related to Internet security. Employees also need the hardware (computers) to have access to their information.

Shared Services and Shared-Services Centers

In this setup, specific processes are outsourced to a third party. Among HR processes that may be included are payroll, procurement, accounts payable and receivable, travel expenses, health benefits enrollment, and pension administration. Under the shared-services model, the administrative functions can be handled in-house or outsourced. Technological advances and increasingly sophisticated use of Internet communications have played a major rule in spurring shared-services arrangements in recent years.

The Decision Process

The process of deciding whether to outsource any HR function should start by considering how outsourcing could help an organization and its HR operations.

In addition, it is important to know the ways in which an outsourcing arrangement can fall short of expectations, and to reduce risks. You should be aware of the main areas of concern for outsourcing:

- Legal and regulatory compliance. Determine exactly what compliance services the outsourcing vendor will provide and whether the vendor's services will completely satisfy your legal obligations in such areas as leave (in the Family and Medical Leave Act), accommodation (in the Americans with Disabilities Act), health care benefits (in the Affordable Care Act), and wage and hour issues (in the Fair Labor Standards Act). This concern is most acute when a state or local requirement is significantly different or more stringent than a comparable federal requirement.
- Service levels. Make certain there is a full understanding of the services to be provided—exactly what the vendor will do and what you will be responsible for doing.
- Process. Providers may carry out tasks in ways that differ from methods familiar to the organization. You must thoroughly understand the vendor's processes and know how your organization may play a role in those processes.

Choosing Functions for Outsourcing

The following are some areas of human resources that are sometimes outsourced and the ways in which they can be outsourced:

- Scope of services and base price. The typical contract contains a fixed price for a base amount of work and a variable price for incremental increases or decreases from the base line.

- Service-level fundamentals. The organization should have a clear understanding of the vendor's performance commitments; the service levels must be explicit and enforceable. Because service levels need to improve over the life of the contract, make sure you have documented the services existing when your contract becomes effective to ensure the vendor has accountability.

- Exit plans. Consider including automatic termination rights in the event of mission-critical, service-level failures or chronic poor performance. Set out a specific set of circumstances in which a termination might automatically come into play if service levels are not being met or if credits exceed a certain amount.

- Additional contract terms. The contract also needs to address control of personnel, including subcontractors; what staff will transition over to the supplier; and the limits on liability.

Outsourcing Vendor Consideration

Decision Worksheet 8.1 (HR Outsourcing) provides a way to track your consideration of vendors.

It is wise to have a final agreement reviewed by your legal counsel.

Managing the Relationship

Outsourcing HR functions can involve significant costs, but outsourcing to a skilled vendor—and using that vendor correctly—can save organizations money in the long run. The key is to manage the relationship well.

DECISION WORKSHEET 8.1. **HR OUTSOURCING**		
Outsourcing for (list HR functions to be outsourced)		
Vendor Name and contact info		
Date		
Item	**Information**	**Check if included**
Service you want to outsource		
Scope of services provided by the vendor, what will be done, when, what information involvement will your staff have to provide		
Pricing, costs, payment terms, expected price increases, etc.		
Exit plans—how can the agreement be ended, how much notice will you need to give, etc.?		
Additional contract terms: •Regulatory compliance •Control of personnel, including subcontractors, and what staff will transition over to the supplier. •Confidentiality agreement related to HR information •Limits on liability, their bonding or insurance, risk.		
Ownership and resources—how will the transition take place and who "owns" employees, equipment, processes, products, etc.		

Final Thoughts

The process of thoroughly analyzing your needs before hiring an HR professional and then following a step-by-step process to hire that person will likely help you get the best match for your organization.

Starting off the relationship well by using an onboarding and orientation process specific to the needs of an HR professional will build a solid relationship and help that person have a better chance for success.

Continuing the strong support and communication process with your HR professional through a reasonable set of goals and a review of the performance against those goals, supported by continuing education and development, will benefit both you and your HR professional.

All of these steps and resources are actually an investment in the future of your organization. The world of business continues to change and move faster, and it depends on your employees. An effective, robust HR function will help your future success.

Endnotes

Chapter 1

1. Society for Human Resource Management (SHRM), *2014 SHRM Learning System for PHR/SPHR Certification Preparation, Module 1: Business Management and Strategy* (Alexandria, VA: SHRM, 2014), ix-xvii.

2. U.S. Equal Employment Opportunity Commission, "Charge Statistics: FY 1997 through FY 2013," http://www.eeoc.gov/eeoc/statistics/enforcement/charges.cfm.

3. U.S. Equal Employment Opportunity Commission, "Newsroom," http://www.eeoc.gov/eeoc/newsroom/index.cfm.

4. U.S. Department of Labor, "Summary of the Major Laws of the Department of Labor," http://www.dol.gov/opa/aboutdol/lawsprog.htm; also see Allen Smith, "DOL Ramps Up Wage and Hour Enforcement," *SHRM Online*, May 11, 2012, http://www.shrm.org/legalissues/federalresources/pages/dolwageandhour.aspx.

5. "Are You Spending Too Much on Payroll?," *Bellevue Business Journal*, December 31, 2013, http://bellevuebusinessjournal.com/2013/12/31/are-you-spending-too-much-on-payroll.

Chapter 2

1. Dori Meinert, "Cultural Similarities Influence Hiring Decisions," *HR Magazine*, February 2013, http://www.shrm.org/publications/hrmagazine/editorialcontent/2013/0213/pages/0213execbrief.aspx.

Chapter 3

1. Society for Human Resource Management, "SHRM Elements for HR Success Competency Model," http://www.shrm.org/HRCompetencies/Pages/Model.aspx.

2. HR Certification Institute, http://www.hrci.org/.

3. Bureau of Labor Statistics, http://www.bls.gov/.

4. Society for Human Resource Management, "Compensation & Benefits e-Newsletter," http://www.shrm.org/hrdisciplines/compensation/Pages/default.aspx.

Chapter 4

1. iHireHR, http://www.ihirehr.com/.

2. Society for Human Resource Management, "SHRM's HR Jobs," http://jobs.shrm.org.

3. Society for Human Resource Management, SHRM Research Spotlight, "HR Professionals' Job Satisfaction and Engagement," January 2014, http://www.shrm.org/Research/SurveyFindings/Articles/Documents/HR-JSE-2013.pdf.

4. USAJOBS, https://www.usajobs.gov/.

5. Society for Human Resource Management, "The Use of Social Networking Websites and Online Search Engines in Screening Job Candidates Survey Findings," August 25, 2011, http://www.shrm.org/research/surveyfindings/articles/pages/theuseofsocialnetworkingwebsitesandonlinesearchenginesinscreeningjobcandidates.aspx.

Chapter 5

1. Wendy Bliss, "Understanding Workplace Cultures Globally," *SHRM Online*, February 1, 2014, http://www.shrm.org/templatestools/toolkits/pages/understandingworkplaceculturesglobally.aspx.

Chapter 8

1. Much of this information is adapted from Angela Collins, "Outsourcing HR," *SHRM Online*, last modified March 2013, http://www.shrm.org/templatestools/toolkits/pages/outsourcingthehrfunction.aspx.

Index

Note: Italicized page numbers refer to references inside of tables and decision worksheets.

D

data management, *50*, 112
defined contribution, 111
discrimination, 61, 73, *83*

E

EEO regulations, 49
EEO-1 report, 49
employee
   communication(s), 29, *32, 38, 82*
   development, *14, 36, 84-5, 108*
   files, *32*
   handbook, *32, 49, 84, 96, 108*
   relations, *14*, 17, 18, *50, 84*
employment firm, 62
employment relationship, *81*, 102
equal employment opportunity (EEO), 15
exempt, *34*, 46, *49*

F

Facebook, 58, 60
Fair Labor Standards Act (FLSA), *83*, 114
Family and Medical Leave Act (FMLA), 29, *83*, 114
feedback, 102
financial data, 96

H

Harris Interactive, 17
health benefits, 111, 115
health plans, 111
hiring decision, 17, 61, 71, 73
hiring process, 33, 56, 96, *107*
HR Certification Institute, *43*, 104
HR certification(s), 39, 41, 43, 45, 104; *see table 3.1*
   Certified Compensation Professional (CCP), *43, 51*, 75, 104
   Certified Employee Benefit Specialist (CEBS), *45*, 104
   Certified Professional in Human Resources and Compensation (CPHRC), *43, 51*, 104
   Certified Professional in Learning and Performance Certification (CPLP), *43, 51*, 104
   Compensation Management Specialist (CMS), *45*, 104
   Global Professional in Human Resources (GPHR), 104
   Human Resource Business Professional (HRBP), 104
   Human Resource Management Professional (HRMP), 104

phone screen, 70, *79; see decision worksheet 5.2*
physicals, 74
planning process, 17, 66

Q
qualifications, 28, 39

R
recognition programs, *34,* 113
records retention, *32,* 112
recruiting, *13,* 41, 55, 56, 58, 60, 61, 62, *63,* 69, *80,* 96
   company, 61, 62
   plan, 62; *see decision worksheet 4.1*
   process, 41, 56, 62, 73, *107*
   recruitment, *13,* 22, 29, *33, 38, 48, 57,* 60, 67, 107
   external, 112
   reference(s), 73, 74
   calls, 74
   checking form, 74; *see decision worksheet 5.5*
   checks, *33,* 66, 72, 73
rejection, *33,* 75
relocation, 68, 112
resume(s), 56, *63, 64,* 66, 67, 68, 69, 73, *78, 79*
   review, 68
risk management, *15,* 29, *85-6,* 103

S
safety, *15, 36, 37, 38, 84, 108,* 113
salary, *14, 37,* 46-7, 56, 61; *see decision worksheet 3.2*
   surveys, 47, 111
Salary.com, 46
screening, 73
   initial, 66, 69
Second Wind Consultants, 16
selection process, *13, 33,* 66
shared services, 114
SHRM Connect, 60
SMART goals, 102
social media, *32,* 58, 61
Society for Human Resource Management (SHRM), 13, 40, *42, 43, 44,* 45, 47, *51, 54,* 55, 58, 60, 69, 75, 103, 104
stakeholders, *51,* 98
strategic plan, *13, 52, 96, 101, 107*
strategic planning, *49, 81*
   process, 17

About the Author

Phyllis G. Hartman, SPHR, is the founder of PGHR Consulting, Inc., and has over 25 years of experience as an HR professional. A frequent speaker on human resources, business, and career development, Phyllis is a member of the Society for Human Resource Management's Ethics and Corporate Social Responsibility and Sustainability expert panel. Phyllis is also a member of the SHRM A-Team providing advocacy for HR legislation.

This is Phyllis' second book. She co-authored with Nancy Glube *Never Get Lost Again: Navigating Your HR Career*, published by SHRM in 2009. She contributes articles to the Applied Behavioral Insights monthly newsletter, which is distributed to small business owners, and has participated in webcasts for the same audience on HR topics. Phyllis has written articles, white papers, and book chapters on HR topics, and she teaches human resources and business courses at several Pittsburgh colleges and universities.

She was the recipient of a Distinguished Alumni Award in 2013 from La Roche College, where she currently teaches HR courses. She has delivered programs at the SHRM Annual Conference, as well as at the PA SHRM State Council; the Utah, Vermont, and Virginia SHRM state councils; SHRM Student Conferences; and local SHRM and business organizations. She has held leadership positions in the Pennsylvania SHRM State Council and the Pittsburgh HR Association.

Phyllis is the vice chair of the Homeless Children's Education in Pittsburgh and participates in several committees to support educational opportunities for children experiencing homelessness.

In her business, Phyllis provides a variety of HR consulting services, including recruitment, outplacement coaching, employee relations consulting, and training to a wide variety of small- and mid-sized organizations. Prior to founding PGHR, she worked as a practitioner in HR management in for-profit manufacturing and nonprofit service sectors.

Phyllis holds a master's in human resource management from La Roche College and a bachelor's in education from Edinboro University of Pennsylvania. Phyllis lives outside of Pittsburgh with her husband, Chuck. She is an active hiker, birdwatcher, puzzle-solver, and reader.

Additional
SHRM-Published Books

The ACE Advantage: How Smart Companies Unleash Talent for Optimal Performance
William A. Schiemann

Becoming the Evidence-Based Manager: Making the Science of Management Work for You
Gary P. Latham

Healthy Employees, Healthy Business: Easy, Affordable Ways to Promote Workplace Wellness
Ilona Bray

Hidden Drivers of Success: Leveraging Employee Insights for Strategic Advantage
William A. Schiemann, Jerry H. Seibert, and Brian S. Morgan

Human Capital Benchmarking
Society for Human Resource Management

Investing in What Matters: Linking Employees to Business Outcomes
Scott P. Mondore and Shane S. Douthitt

A Necessary Evil: Managing Employee Activity on Facebook, Twitter, LinkedIn ... and the Hundreds of Other Social Media Sites
Aliah D. Wright

Point Counterpoint: New Perspectives on People & Strategy
Anna Tavis, Richard Vosburgh, and Ed Gubman

All of SHRM's books and e-books can be found at www.shrm.org/publications/books/pages/shrm-publishedbooks(alphalist).aspx.